First published 2016 by

Elmwood Education Ltd
Unit 5, Mallow Park
Watchmead
Welwyn Garden City
Herts. AL7 1GX
Tel. 01707 333232

All rights reserved. No part of this publication may be reproduced, stored in a retrieval system, or transmitted, in any form or by any means, electronic, mechanical, photocopying, recording or otherwise, without permission in writing from the publisher or under licence from the Copyright Licensing Agency, Saffron House, 6–10 Kirby Street, London EC1N 8TS.

Any person who commits any unauthorised act in relation to this publication may be liable to criminal prosecution and civil claims for damages.

© Stephen Pearce
The moral rights of the authors have been asserted.
Database right Elmwood Education (maker)

ISBN 9781 906 622 619.

Typeset by Tech-Set Ltd., Gateshead, Tyne and Wear.
Illustrated by Stephen Hill.
Email: hilly.moto@btinternet.com
Printed in the UK by TJ International Ltd, Padstow, Cornwall

PREFACE

Target your Maths has been written for pupils in Year 1 and their teachers.

The intention of this workbook is to provide teachers with material to teach the statutory requirements set out in the Year 1 Programme of Study for Mathematics in the renewed 2014 National Curriculum Framework. The Programme of Study Guide matches the statutory requirements with the relevant page or pages.

Each lesson in the book is divided into three sections.

Section A: introductory activities which develop towards the requirements for Year 1 pupils. This section can be used to remind children of work previously encountered in Reception, as well as providing material for the less confident child.

Section B: activities based upon the requirements for Year 1 pupils. Most children should be able to work successfully at this level.

Section C: activities providing extension material for the faster workers and for those who need to be moved quickly onto more challenging tasks. The work generally matches the requirements for Year 2 pupils. Problems in Section C can also provide useful material for discussion in the plenary session.

The correspondence of the three sections A−C to the requirements for different year groups provides a simple, manageable structure for planning differentiated activities and for both the formal and informal assessment of children's progress. The commonality of the content pitched at different levels also allows for progression within the lesson. Children acquiring confidence at one level find they can successfully complete activities at the next level.

Target your Maths has been organised into a three term school year. Each term there are activities covering statutory requirements in each of the six domains in the renewed Framework. The Number and Measurement domains are revisited within each term, whereas Fractions and Geometry are dealt with as discrete topics. There is, of course, no set path through either the Year 1 Programme of Study or Target your Maths but teachers may find the approach used in this workbook useful for planning purposes.

The author is indebted to many colleagues who have assisted him in this work. He is particularly grateful to Sharon Granville and Davina Tunkel for their invaluable assistance and advice.

Stephen Pearce

Year 1 NC Programme of Study Guide

> **THE REFERENCES ARE PAGE NUMBERS IN TARGET YOUR MATHS**

NUMBER AND PLACE VALUE

1, 25, 50	count to and across 100, forwards and backwards, beginning with 0 or 1, or from any given number.
11, 34, 35, 51, 56	count, read and write numbers to 100 in numerals; count in multiples of twos, fives and tens.
3	given a number, identify one more and one less.
10, 27	identify and represent numbers using objects and pictorial representations including the number line, and use the language of: equal to, more than, less than (fewer), most, least.
2, 26	read and write numbers from 1 to 20 in numerals and words.

ADDITION AND SUBTRACTION

4, 5, 12, 13, 28, 30, 36, 38, 46, 52, 53, 58	read, write and interpret mathematical statements involving addition (+), subtraction (−) and equals (=) signs.
4, 5, 12, 13, 28, 30, 36, 46, 52, 58	represent and use number bonds and related subtraction facts within 20.
4, 5, 12, 13, 28, 30, 36, 46, 52, 58	add and subtract one-digit and two digit numbers to 20, including zero.
6, 14, 21, 22, 29, 37, 38, 47, 53, 59, 69, 70	solve one-step problems that involve addition and subtraction, using concrete objects and pictorial representations, and missing number problems such as $7 = \square - 9$.

MULTIPLICATION AND DIVISION

17, 18, 42, 43, 64–66	solve one-step problems involving multiplication and division, by calculating the answer using concrete objects, pictorial representations and arrays with the support of the teacher.

FRACTIONS

19, 20, 67	recognise, find and name a half as one of two equal parts of an object, shape or quantity.
44, 45, 68	recognise, find and name a quarter as one of four equal parts of an object, shape or quantity.

MEASUREMENT

Compare, describe and solve practical problems for:

7	lengths and heights (for example, long/short, longer/shorter, tall/short, double/half)
31	mass/weight (for example, heavy/light, heavier than, lighter than)
54	capacity and volume (for example, full/empty, more than, less than, half, half full, quarter)
72	time (for example, quicker, slower, earlier, later)

Measure and begin to record the following:

8, 9	lengths and heights
32, 33	mass/weight
55	capacity and volume
49, 71	time (hours, minutes, seconds)
39, 60	recognise and know the value of different denominations of coins and notes
23	sequence events in chronological order using language (for example, before and after, next, first, today, yesterday, tomorrow, morning, afternoon and evening)
24, 48	recognise and use language relating to dates, including days of the week, weeks months and years
49, 71, 72	tell the time to the hour and half past the hour and draw the hands on a clock face to show these times.

GEOMETRY

Recognise and name common 2-D and 3-D shapes, including:

15, 16	2-D shapes (for example, rectangles (including squares), circles and triangles)
40, 41	3-D shapes (for example, cuboids (including cubes), pyramids and spheres)
61–63	describe position, direction and movement, including whole, half, quarter and three-quarter turns

Year 1

CONTENTS

TERM 1
Counting 1	1
Reading and Writing Numbers 1	2
One More, One Less	3
Addition Facts 1	4
Adding 10	5
Addition Problems 1	6
Comparing Lengths	7
Measuring Lengths 1	8
Measuring Lengths 2	9
Comparing Numbers	10
Counting in Twos	11
Subtraction Facts 1	12
Subtracting 10	13
Subtraction Problems 1	14
Describing 2-D Shapes	15
2-D Shapes	16
Arrays 1	17
Grouping 1	18
Halves of Lines	19
Halves of Shapes	20
Addition Word Problems	21
Subtraction Word Problems	22
Ordering Events	23
Days of the Week	24

TERM 2
Counting 2	25
Reading and Writing Numbers 2	26
Using Number Lines	27
Addition Facts 2	28
Addition Problems 2	29
Making Totals 1	30
Comparing Weights	31
Measuring Weight 1	32
Measuring Weight 2	33
Counting in Fives	34
Counting in Tens	35
Subtraction Facts 2	36
Subtraction Problems 2	37
Missing Number Problems 1	38
Recognising Coins	39
3-D Shapes	40
Describing 3-D Shapes	41
Arrays 2	42
Grouping 2	43
Halves and Quarters of Lines	44
Halves and Quarters of Shapes	45
Making Totals 2	46
+/− Problems 1	47
Months of the Year	48
Clocks 1	49

TERM 3
First, Second, Third...	50
Place Value	51
+/− Facts 1	52
Dice	53
Comparing Capacities	54
Measuring Capacity	55
Counting in Groups	56
Odd and Even Numbers	57
+/− Facts 2	58
Finding Differences	59
Recognising Notes and Coins	60
Positions	61
Directions	62
Turns	63
Doubling and Halving	64
Multiplying Problems	65
Dividing Problems	66
Fractions of Quantities 1	67
Fractions of Quantities 2	68
Missing Number Problems 2	69
+/− Problems 2	70
Clocks 2	71
Comparing Times	72

Sheet 1 COUNTING 1

Fill in the boxes.

A

3 4 5 ☐ ☐ | 7 count on 5 ☐ | 19 count back 4 ☐
12 11 10 ☐ ☐ | 13 count on 4 ☐ | 13 count back 7 ☐
14 15 16 ☐ ☐ | 9 count on 2 ☐ | 17 count back 6 ☐
20 19 18 ☐ ☐ | 15 count on 5 ☐ | 14 count back 5 ☐
11 12 13 ☐ ☐ | 12 count on 6 ☐ | 20 count back 3 ☐

0 1 2 3 4 5 6 7 8 9 10 11 12 13 14 15 16 17 18 19 20

B

          Count on   Count back

23 24 25 ☐ ☐ | 5 from 74 ☐ | 6 from 42 ☐
50 49 48 ☐ ☐ | 4 from 39 ☐ | 3 from 80 ☐
89 90 91 ☐ ☐ | 6 from 64 ☐ | 9 from 54 ☐
42 41 40 ☐ ☐ | 7 from 25 ☐ | 6 from 23 ☐
96 97 98 ☐ ☐ | 9 from 91 ☐ | 7 from 71 ☐

0 10 20 30 40 50 60 70 80 90 100

C

          Count on   Count back

122 123 124 ☐ ☐ | 7 from 159 ☐ | 6 from 123 ☐
103 102 101 ☐ ☐ | 5 from 98 ☐ | 7 from 170 ☐
176 177 178 ☐ ☐ | 6 from 184 ☐ | 5 from 104 ☐
142 141 140 ☐ ☐ | 5 from 106 ☐ | 6 from 151 ☐
97 98 99 ☐ ☐ | 8 from 94 ☐ | 8 from 102 ☐

Sheet 2 READING AND WRITING NUMBERS 1

A

Write in figures.

one	1
two	
three	
four	
five	
six	
seven	
eight	
nine	
ten	

Write in words.

3 ..... three
8 .....
5 .....
7 .....
2 .....
9 .....
4 .....
10 .....
6 .....

B

Write in figures.

eleven	
twelve	
thirteen	
fourteen	
fifteen	
sixteen	
seventeen	
eighteen	
nineteen	
twenty	

Write in words.

14 .....
19 .....
12 .....
15 .....
17 .....
11 .....
20 .....
13 .....
18 .....

C

Write in figures.

ten	
twenty	
thirty	
forty	
fifty	
sixty	
seventy	
eighty	
ninety	
one hundred	

Write in words.

43 ..... forty-three
79 .....
64 .....
27 .....
92 .....
36 .....
58 .....
81 .....
45 .....

Sheet 3 ONE MORE, ONE LESS

A

one more	one less	one more	one less
3 [4]	8 [7]	9 [ ]	1 [ ]
18 [ ]	10 [ ]	6 [ ]	13 [ ]
10 [ ]	5 [ ]	11 [ ]	18 [ ]
1 [ ]	16 [ ]	8 [ ]	6 [ ]
16 [ ]	3 [ ]	14 [ ]	14 [ ]

B

Fill in the boxes.

27 + 1 = 28   59 − 1 =   98 + 1 =   42 − 1 =

62 + 1 =   43 − 1 =   40 + 1 =   35 − 1 =

74 + 1 =   97 − 1 =   83 + 1 =   86 − 1 =

39 + 1 =   24 − 1 =   51 + 1 =   71 − 1 =

85 + 1 =   70 − 1 =   26 + 1 =   68 − 1 =

C

Fill in the boxes.

153 + 1 =   176 − 1 =   275 + 1 =   741 − 1 =

116 + 1 =   164 − 1 =   520 + 1 =   315 − 1 =

181 + 1 =   199 − 1 =   388 + 1 =   233 − 1 =

129 + 1 =   132 − 1 =   604 + 1 =   987 − 1 =

192 + 1 =   108 − 1 =   457 + 1 =   200 − 1 =

Sheet 4 ADDITION FACTS 1

Fill in the boxes.

A

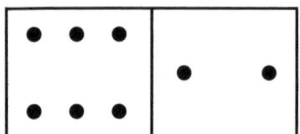
6 + 2 = 8

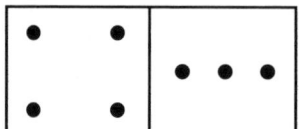
☐ + ☐ = ☐

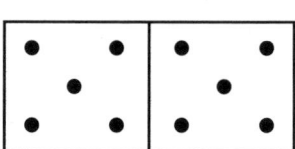
☐ + ☐ = ☐

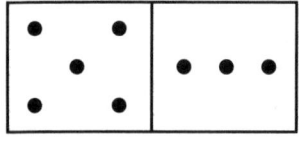
☐ + ☐ = ☐

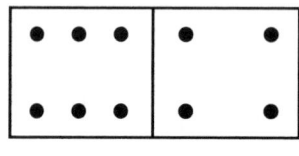
☐ + ☐ = ☐

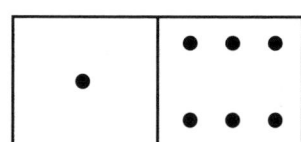
☐ + ☐ = ☐

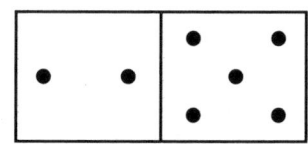
☐ + ☐ = ☐

☐ + ☐ = ☐

☐ + ☐ = ☐

B

8 + 5 = 13   8 + 8 = ☐   5 + 9 = ☐   5 + 7 = ☐

7 + 9 = ☐   7 + 4 = ☐   6 + 6 = ☐   9 + 9 = ☐

6 + 7 = ☐   6 + 5 = ☐   4 + 8 = ☐   8 + 6 = ☐

7 + 3 = ☐   8 + 7 = ☐   9 + 6 = ☐   9 + 8 = ☐

C

16 + 9 = ☐   18 + 6 = ☐   15 + 9 = ☐   17 + 8 = ☐

15 + 7 = ☐   14 + 8 = ☐   19 + 8 = ☐   16 + 7 = ☐

13 + 8 = ☐   17 + 7 = ☐   17 + 5 = ☐   18 + 9 = ☐

19 + 4 = ☐   16 + 5 = ☐   18 + 3 = ☐   19 + 6 = ☐

Sheet 5 ADDING 10

A Here are 16 counters.
Colour 10 red.
Colour the rest blue.
Fill in the boxes.

○ ○ ○ ○ ○ ○ ○ ○
○ ○ ○ ○ ○ ○ ○

10 + ☐ = 16
red   blue

Here are 13 counters.
Colour 10 red.
Colour the rest blue.
Fill in the boxes.

○ ○ ○ ○ ○ ○ ○
○ ○ ○ ○ ○ ○

☐ + ☐ = ☐
red   blue

B Fill in the boxes.

2 + 10 = 12   ☐ + 10 = 16   3 + 10 = ☐
7 + 10 = ☐   ☐ + 10 = 12   6 + 10 = ☐
4 + 10 = ☐   ☐ + 10 = 15   1 + 10 = ☐
0 + 10 = ☐   ☐ + 10 = 19   8 + 10 = ☐
9 + 10 = ☐   ☐ + 10 = 11   5 + 10 = ☐

C Fill in the boxes.

24 + 10 = 34   42 + 10 = ☐   65 + 10 = ☐
58 + 10 = ☐   79 + 10 = ☐   37 + 10 = ☐
63 + 10 = ☐   51 + 10 = ☐   43 + 10 = ☐
87 + 10 = ☐   26 + 10 = ☐   59 + 10 = ☐
35 + 10 = ☐   84 + 10 = ☐   72 + 10 = ☐

Sheet 6 ADDITION PROBLEMS 1

Fill in the boxes.

A

6 add 2 = 8   1 and 8 make ☐   2 and 8 together ☐

3 add 3 = ☐   4 and 3 make ☐   7 and 0 together ☐

5 add 4 = ☐   8 and 1 make ☐   4 and 5 together ☐

7 add 3 = ☐   3 and 5 make ☐   1 and 6 together ☐

2 add 4 = ☐   6 and 4 make ☐   5 and 5 together ☐

B

What is 6 and 8 altogether? ☐   8 more than 3 ☐

The total of 13 and 3 is ☐   4 more than 15 ☐

9 and 9 equals ☐   10 more than 6 ☐

Altogether 5 and 6 make ☐   3 more than 14 ☐

What is 7 add 3? ☐   12 more than 8 ☐

11 and 4 have a total of ☐   5 more than 13 ☐

C

5, 7 and 9 make ☐   8 plus 13 ☐

The sum of 24 and 7 is ☐   25 plus 10 ☐

19 is 6 greater than ☐   14 plus 9 ☐

The total of 17, 5 and 10 is ☐   40 plus 60 ☐

Add 20, 30 and 40. ☐   11 plus 11 ☐

20 more than 15 is ☐   8 plus 16 ☐

Sheet 7 COMPARING LENGTHS

A
Colour the pictures.

long → red
short → yellow

tall → red
short → yellow

high → red
low → yellow

B
Colour the pictures.

long → shorter → shortest
red → orange → yellow

narrow → wider → widest
yellow → orange → red

thick → thinner → thinnest
red → orange → yellow

C
Fill in the boxes.

glass   12 cm tall
bottle   25 cm tall
The glass is ☐ cm shorter.

hall   15 m wide
classroom   8 m wide
The hall is ☐ m wider.

rope   12 m long
string   8 m long
The rope is ☐ m longer.

tree   11 m tall
house   16 m tall
The house is ☐ m taller.

ruler   30 cm long
pencil   16 cm long
The pencil is ☐ cm shorter.

road   30 m wide
bridge   50 m wide
The road is ☐ m more narrow.

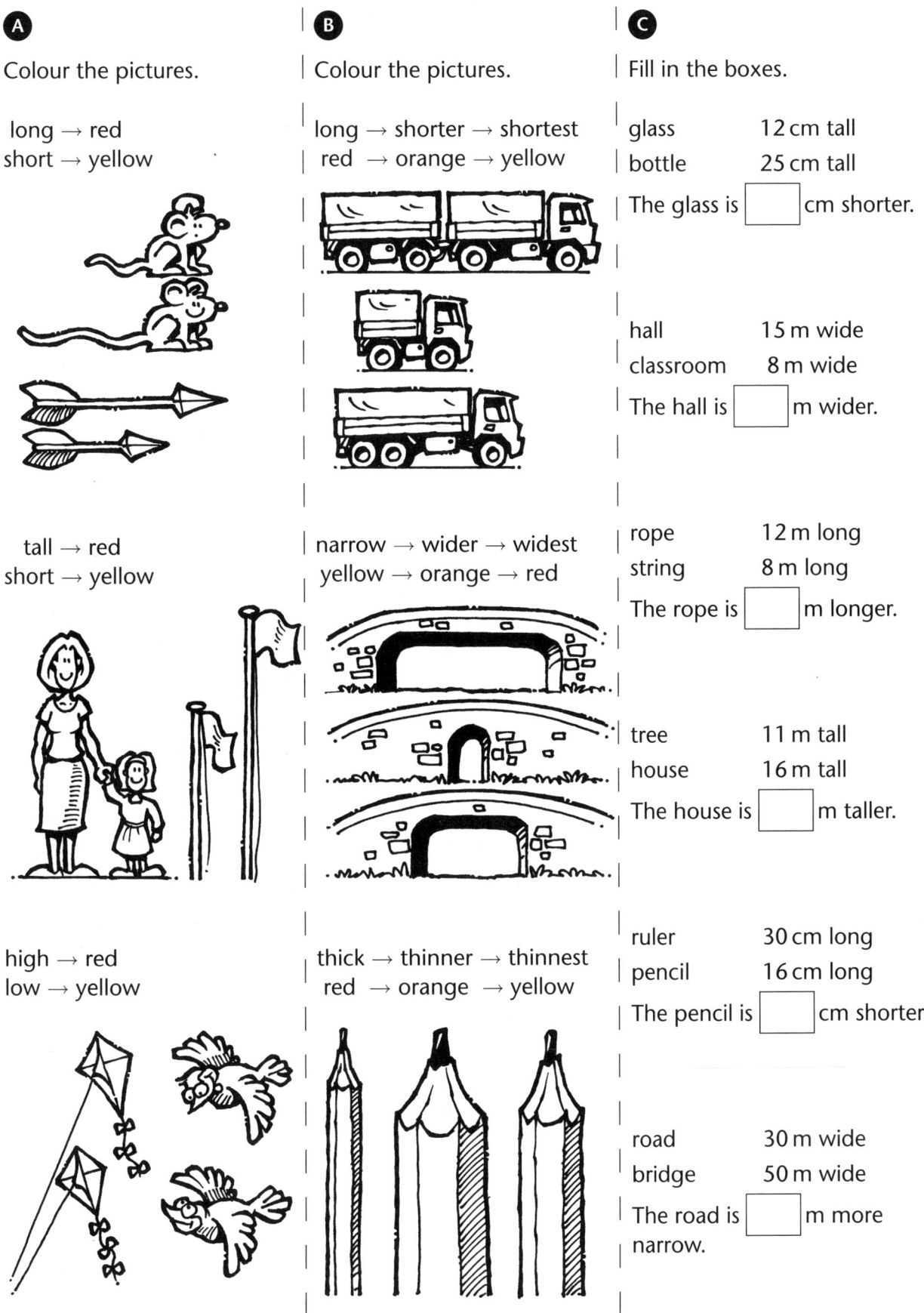

Sheet 8 MEASURING LENGTHS 1

A

Draw something that is about:

5 cubes long	3 pencils long	1 metre stick long

B

Use a metre stick.

The door is about:

......1...... metre stick wide.

.... metre sticks tall.

The classroom is about:

.... metre sticks wide.

.... metre sticks long.

Use a ruler.

My table is about:

.... rulers wide.

.... rulers long.

My bookcase is about:

.... rulers wide.

.... rulers tall.

C

Fill in the boxes.

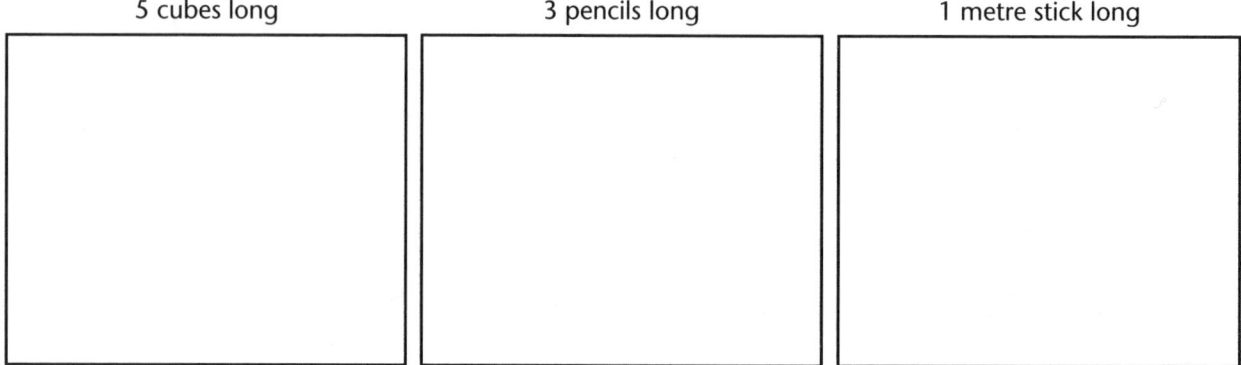

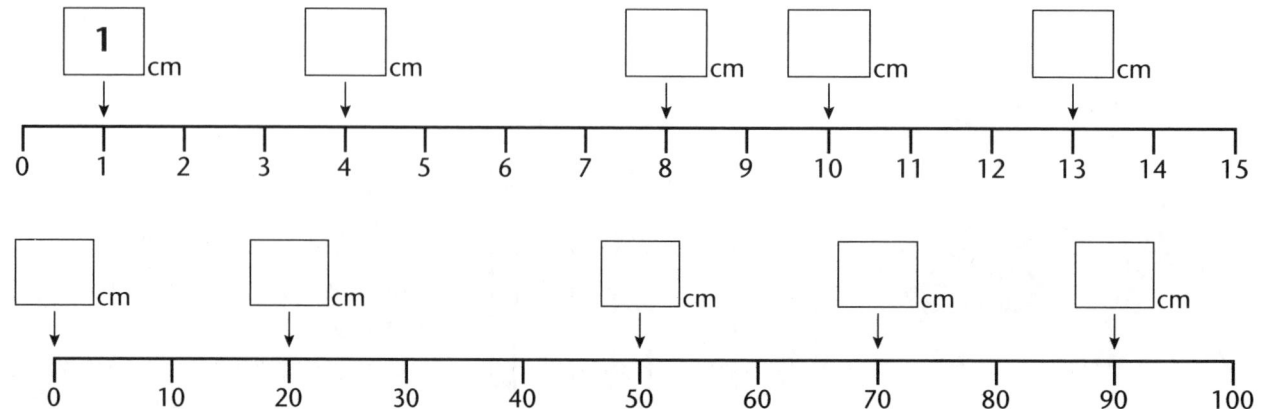

Sheet 9 MEASURING LENGTHS 2

A

Draw something that is about:

1 metre long	half a metre long	20 cm long

B

Fill in the boxes.

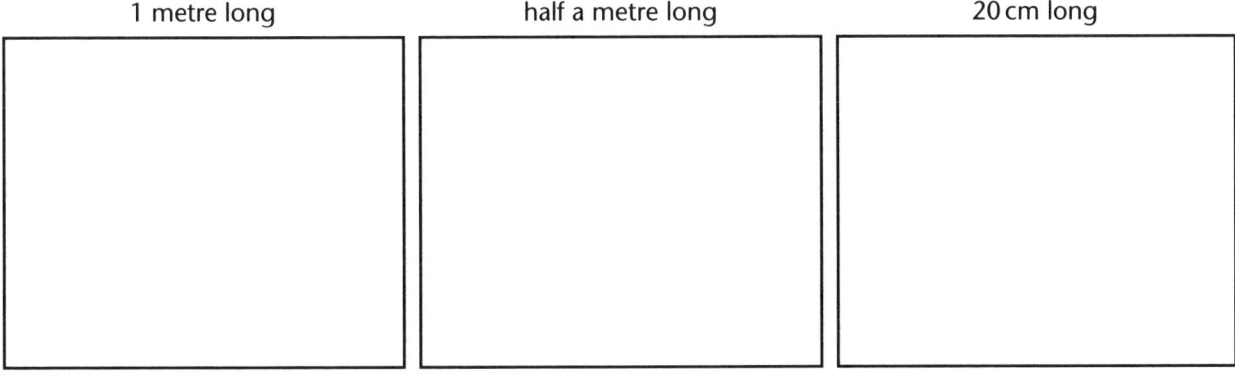

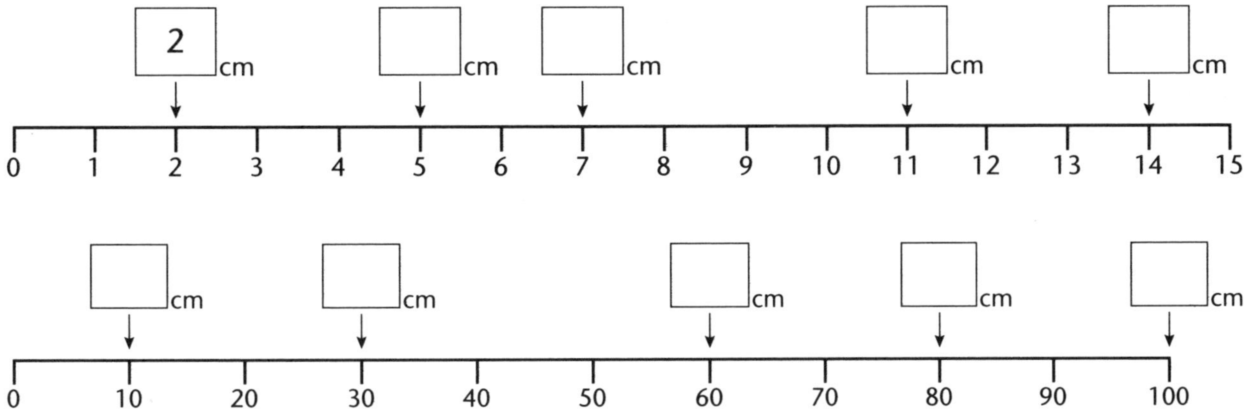

C

Fill in the boxes.

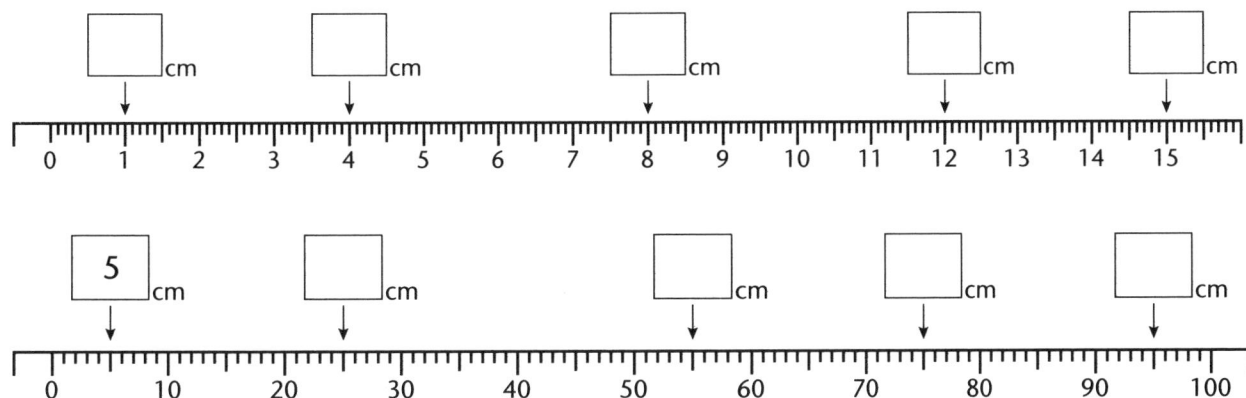

Sheet 10 COMPARING NUMBERS

A

Colour the bigger number.

7	or	12	11	or	8
14	or	15	16	or	18
9	or	13	5	or	10
20	or	19	21	or	17

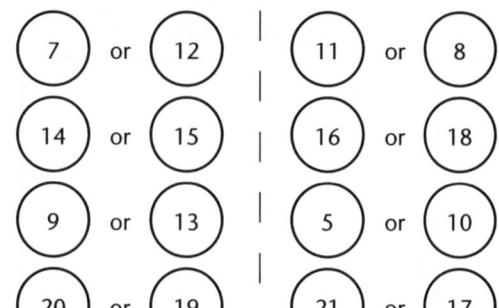

Write the missing number.

5	6	7	10		12
13		15	7		9
9		11	16		18
18		20	12		14

B

Colour the larger number.

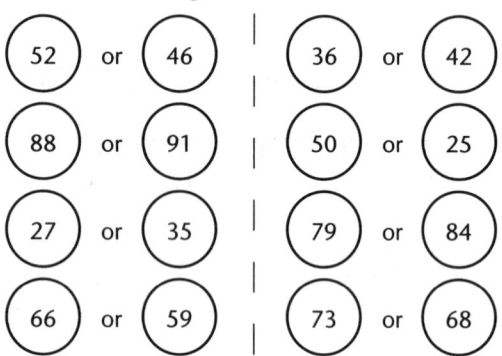

52	or	46	36	or	42
88	or	91	50	or	25
27	or	35	79	or	84
66	or	59	73	or	68

Write the halfway number.

0		4	8		14
8		10	12		20
10		20	9		11
5		9	0		12

C

Largest red, smallest yellow.

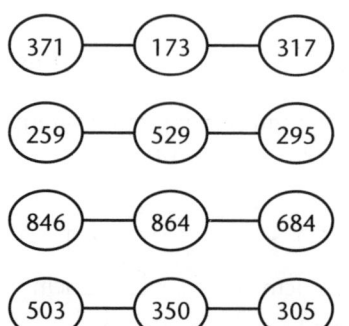

371 — 173 — 317

259 — 529 — 295

846 — 864 — 684

503 — 350 — 305

Write the halfway number.

0		100	15		35
40		80	0		50
50		60	10		70
30		50	50		100

Sheet 11   COUNTING IN TWOS

A

Write the numbers.

two [2]   twelve [ ]

four [ ]   fourteen [ ]

six [ ]   sixteen [ ]

eight [ ]   eighteen [ ]

ten [ ]   twenty [ ]

Write the words.

2 .....two.....   12 ....

4 ....   14 ....

6 ....   16 ....

8 ....   18 ....

10 ....   20 ....

B

Fill in the boxes.

2   4   6   [ ] [ ]

10 12 14 [ ] [ ]

6   8   10 [ ] [ ]

12 14 16 [ ] [ ]

16 18 20 [ ] [ ]

Count on.

3 twos from 4   [10]

5 twos from 14 [ ]

6 twos from 8   [ ]

4 twos from 0   [ ]

3 twos from 12 [ ]

Count on.

5 twos from 6   [ ]

4 twos from 4   [ ]

6 twos from 0   [ ]

3 twos from 16 [ ]

7 twos from 10 [ ]

C

Fill in the boxes.

60 62 64 [ ] [ ]

26 28 30 [ ] [ ]

72 74 76 [ ] [ ]

48 50 52 [ ] [ ]

94 96 98 [ ] [ ]

Count on.

6 twos from 32 [ ]

4 twos from 88 [ ]

5 twos from 56 [ ]

7 twos from 60 [ ]

3 twos from 94 [ ]

Count on.

8 twos from 28 [ ]

5 twos from 40 [ ]

3 twos from 78 [ ]

6 twos from 96 [ ]

4 twos from 34 [ ]

Sheet 12 SUBTRACTION FACTS 1

A

Cross out the circles you will take away. Fill in the box.

10 − 4 = 6

8 − 3 =

7 − 5 =

9 − 5 =

10 − 7 =

8 − 6 =

7 − 3 =

9 − 2 =

10 − 5 =

B

12 − 7 = 5   13 − 5 =   17 − 8 =   15 − 9 =

15 − 8 =   20 − 8 =   12 − 4 =   20 − 11 =

19 − 6 =   11 − 6 =   14 − 6 =   16 − 7 =

14 − 9 =   16 − 9 =   18 − 5 =   11 − 4 =

C

23 − 7 =   25 − 7 =   22 − 6 =   28 − 9 =

22 − 9 =   24 − 8 =   21 − 8 =   25 − 6 =

26 − 8 =   23 − 4 =   26 − 9 =   22 − 3 =

21 − 5 =   27 − 9 =   24 − 5 =   23 − 8 =

Sheet 13 SUBTRACTING 10

A In each group, colour 10 counters red and colour the rest blue. Fill in the boxes.

15 counters    12 counters    18 counters

15 − [10] = [ ]   12 − [ ] = [ ]   18 − [ ] = [ ]
    red blue   red blue   red blue

B Fill in the boxes.

13 − 10 = [3]   [ ] − 10 = 5   16 − 10 = [ ]

12 − 10 = [ ]   [ ] − 10 = 6   11 − 10 = [ ]

19 − 10 = [ ]   [ ] − 10 = 0   20 − 10 = [ ]

14 − 10 = [ ]   [ ] − 10 = 8   15 − 10 = [ ]

17 − 10 = [ ]   [ ] − 10 = 2   18 − 10 = [ ]

C Fill in the boxes.

37 − 10 = [ ]   85 − 10 = [ ]   41 − 10 = [ ]

91 − 10 = [ ]   52 − 10 = [ ]   26 − 10 = [ ]

68 − 10 = [ ]   94 − 10 = [ ]   73 − 10 = [ ]

23 − 10 = [ ]   100 − 10 = [ ]   58 − 10 = [ ]

46 − 10 = [ ]   39 − 10 = [ ]   62 − 10 = [ ]

Sheet 14   SUBTRACTION PROBLEMS 1   14

Fill in the boxes.

A
8 take 3 ☐   Take 3 from 6 ☐   10 take 8 ☐
5 take 4 ☐   Take 6 from 8 ☐   7 take 3 ☐
10 take 5 ☐ Take 7 from 7 ☐   8 take 0 ☐
7 take 1 ☐   Take 1 from 10 ☐ 9 take 4 ☐
9 take 6 ☐   Take 2 from 5 ☐   10 take 6 ☐
10 take 7 ☐ Take 8 from 9 ☐   8 take 2 ☐

B
The difference between 15 and 8 is ☐.   3 less than 11 ☐
6 is ☐ less than 20.   5 less than 17 ☐
Take away 9 from 13. ☐   9 less than 14 ☐
Find the difference between 9 and 18. ☐   11 less than 20 ☐
What is 5 fewer than 16? ☐   0 less than 15 ☐
How many is 12 take 7? ☐   8 less than 19 ☐

C
Subtract 9 from 32. ☐   27 minus 10 ☐
What is the difference between 45 and 38? ☐   60 minus 40 ☐
How many is 80 take away 50? ☐   100 minus 30 ☐
74 minus 6 is ☐.   53 minus 8 ☐
60 less than 100 is ☐.   90 minus 70 ☐
Take 4 from 51 ☐.   48 minus 20 ☐

Sheet 15   DESCRIBING 2-D SHAPES   15

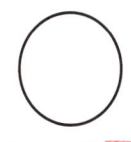 circle → red   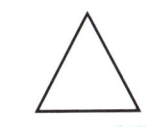 triangle → green    square → blue   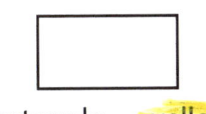 rectangle → yellow

A

Colour the shapes in the pictures.

 house    tree   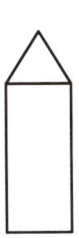 pencil    snowman    sweet

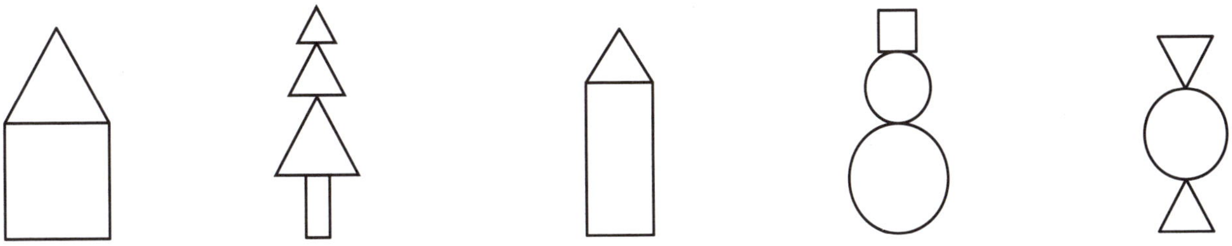

B

Look at the pictures. Fill in the spaces.

house →	1. ......square......	1. ......triangle......
tree →	3.	1. ....
pencil →	1.	1. ....
snowman →	2.	1. ....
sweet →	2.	1. ....

C

Colour in squares to make the shapes.

Find 4 different hexagons (6 sides)   Find 4 different octagons (8 sides)

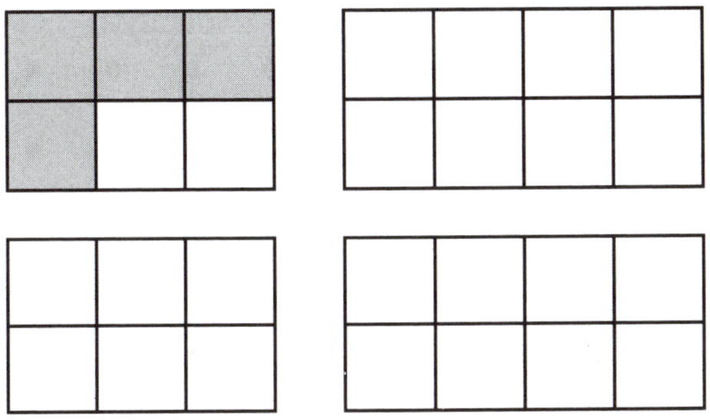

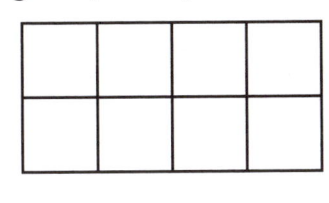 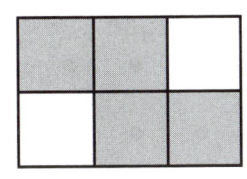 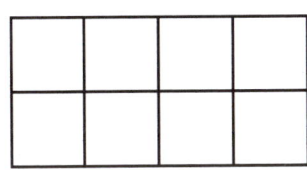

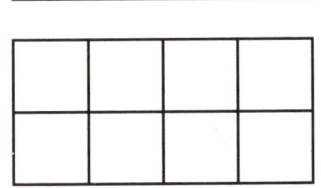 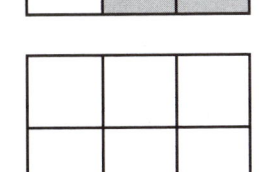 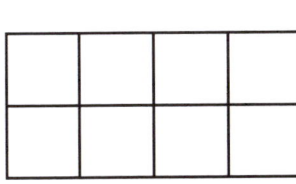

Sheet 16 2-D SHAPES

A

Colour

 red

 blue

△ yellow

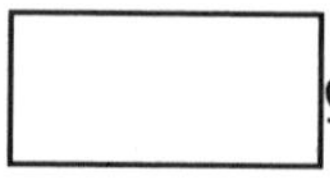

▭ green

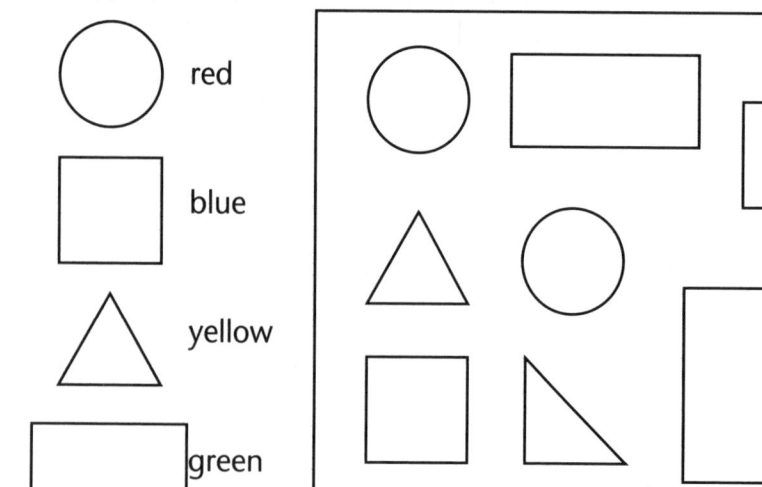

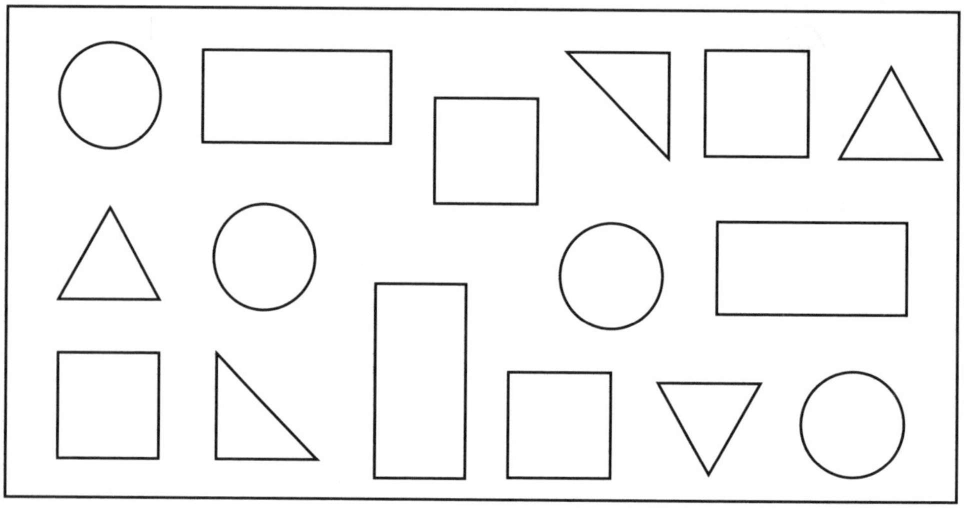

B

Look at the shapes in the box above.

How many?

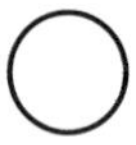

○ circles [4]
□ squares [ ]
△ triangles [ ]
▭ rectangles [ ]

How many sides?

□ [4] sides
△ [ ] sides
▭ [ ] sides

How many corners?

△ [3] corners
▭ [ ] corners
○ [ ] corners
□ [ ] corners

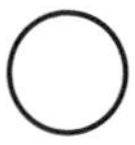

C

Finish the shapes.

rectangle
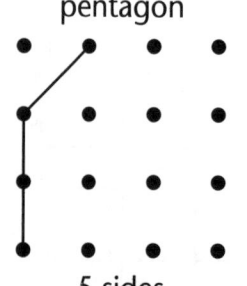
4 sides
4 corners

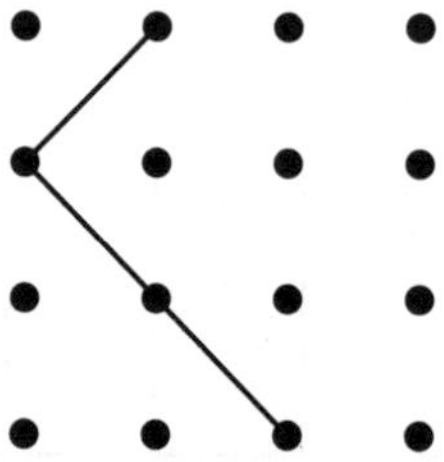

pentagon
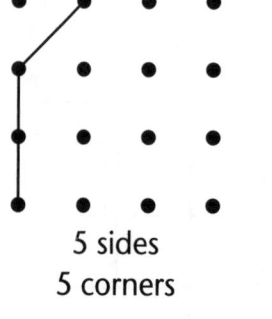
5 sides
5 corners

hexagon
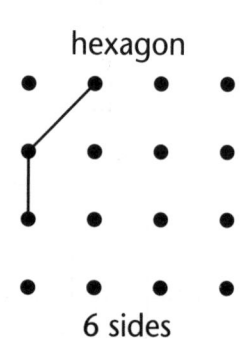
6 sides
6 corners

octagon
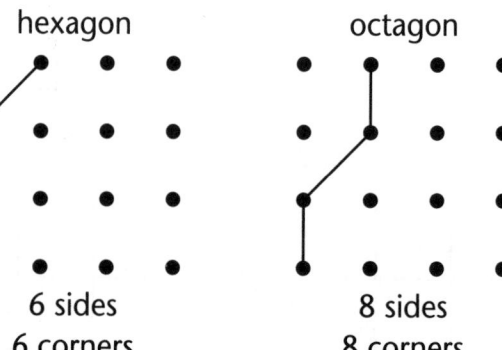
8 sides
8 corners

Sheet 17   ARRAYS 1

Group the dots and fill in the boxes.

A

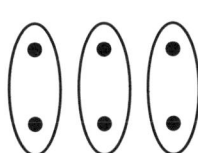

2 + 2 + 2 = 6

3 lots of 2 =

B

2 + 2 + 2 + 2 =

4 lots of 2 =

C

6 lots of 2 =

6 × 2 =

4 + 4 =

2 lots of 4 =

5 + 5 =

2 lots of 5 =

3 lots of 4 =

3 × 4 =

2 + 2 + 2 + 2 + 2 =

5 lots of 2 =

6 + 6 + 6 =

3 lots of 6 =

5 lots of 3 =

5 × 3 =

3 + 3 =

2 lots of 3 =

3 + 3 + 3 + 3 =

4 lots of 3 =

3 lots of 7 =

3 × 7 =

Sheet 18 GROUPING 1

Group the counters. Fill in the boxes.

A

Group into 2s.

10 is [5] groups of 2.

Group into 3s.

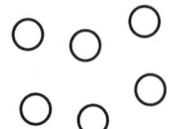

6 is [ ] groups of 3.

Group into 4s.

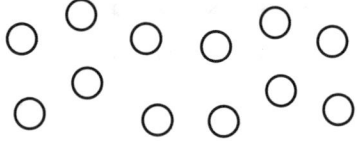

12 is [ ] groups of 4.

Group into 2s.

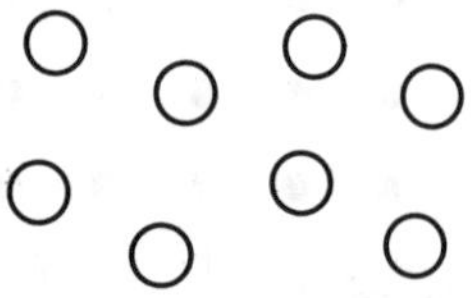

8 is [ ] groups of 2.

B

Group into 2s.

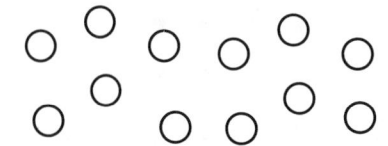

12 is [ ] groups of 2.

Group into 3s.

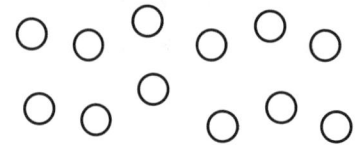

12 is [ ] groups of 3.

Group into 5s.

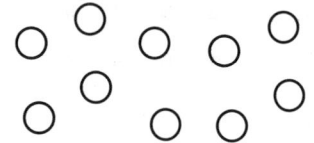

10 is [ ] groups of 5.

Group into 4s.

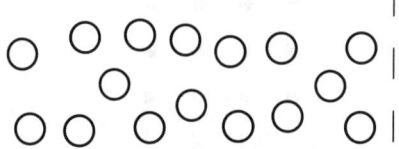

16 is [ ] groups of 4.

C

Group into 3s.

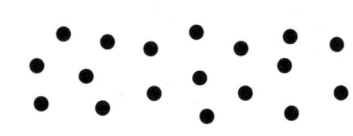

18 is [ ] groups of 3.

Group into 2s.

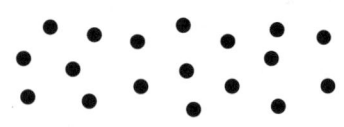

18 is [ ] groups of 2.

Group into 4s.

24 is [ ] groups of 4.

Group into 5s.

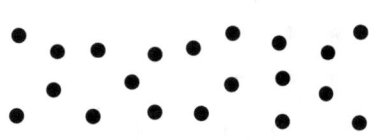

20 is [ ] groups of 5.

Sheet 19   HALVES OF LINES

A

Colour one half of each bar.

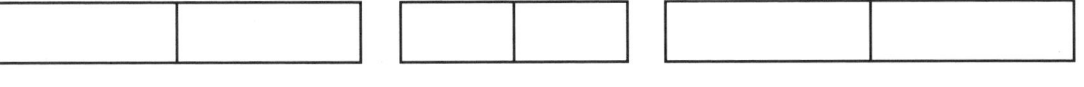

B

Label each half of the line. Write $\frac{1}{2}$ at the halfway mark.

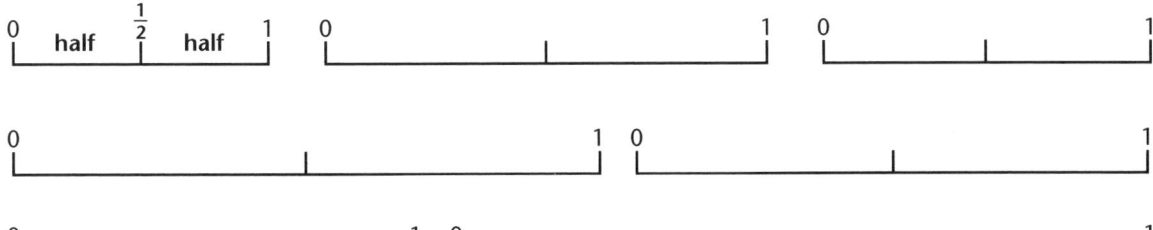

C

Label each quarter by writing qtr. Write $\frac{1}{4}$, $\frac{1}{2}$ or $\frac{3}{4}$ at the marks.

Sheet 20 HALVES OF SHAPES

A

Colour one half of each shape.

B

Use a ruler. Draw a line to make 2 equal halves. Label each $\frac{1}{2}$.

C

Use a ruler. Draw another line to make 4 equal quarters. Label each $\frac{1}{4}$.

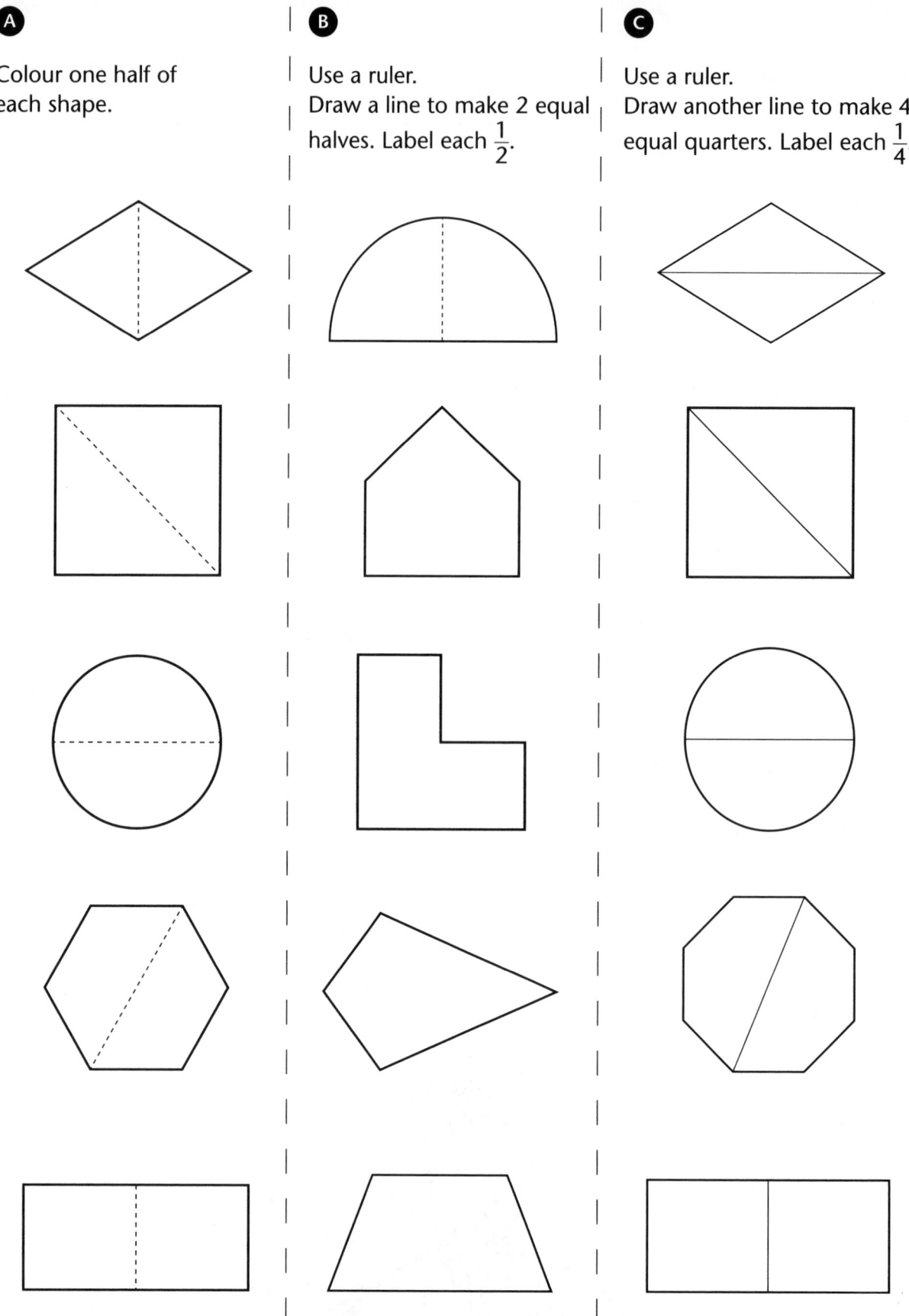

Sheet 21   ADDITION WORD PROBLEMS

Fill in the boxes.

A

4 red apples.   3 green apples.   ☐ apples altogether.

Ben has 5 stars.   He wins 4 more.   He has ☐ stars.

6 blue crayons.   2 yellow crayons.   ☐ crayons altogether.

B

6 boys.
7 girls.
☐ children.

10 books in one pile.
8 books in another pile.
☐ books altogether.

Gina has 15p.
Cassie has 5p.
They have ☐ altogether.

4 glasses of orange.
9 glasses of cola.
☐ drinks altogether.

C

40 brown cows.
30 black and white cows.
☐ cows altogether.

20 people downstairs on the bus..
14 people upstairs on the bus.
☐ people on the bus.

Ravi weighs 25kg.
Dan weighs 7kg more.
Dan weighs ☐ kg.

50 story books.
35 topic books.
☐ books altogether.

Sheet 22 SUBTRACTION WORD PROBLEMS

Fill in the boxes.

A

7 sweets
4 are eaten
☐ sweets left.

6 balloons
2 burst
☐ balloons left.

Nita has 8p
She spends 5p
she has ☐ p left.

B

12 eggs in a box.
5 are eaten.
☐ eggs left.

15m of rope.
10m cut off.
☐ m left.

17 people on a bus.
8 get off.
☐ people on the bus.

20 slices of bread.
16 slices used.
☐ slices left.

C

Micky has £1.
Tony has 40p less.
Tony has ☐ p.

75 cars in a car park.
20 leave.
☐ cars left.

23 adults.
8 are men.
☐ are women.

32 chocolates in a box.
5 chocolates are eaten.
☐ chocolates left.

Sheet 23 ORDERING EVENTS

A

Today is

Yesterday was

Tomorrow will be

Draw something you do every

morning   afternoon

B

The day after tomorrow is   ....

The day before yesterday was   ....

The first school day of the week is   ....

The last school day of the week is   ....

Sue is 6. Next year she will be   ....

Lunchtime comes between the morning and the   ....

C

Write the day before:

Wednesday   ....

Sunday   ....

Monday   ....

Thursday   ....

Saturday   ....

Write the month after:

January   ....

April   ....

November   ....

July   ....

September   ....

Sheet 24 DAYS OF THE WEEK

A

Write the days of the week in the correct order.

Friday
Wednesday
Sunday
Monday
Thursday
Tuesday
Saturday

Day 1 ......Monday...... Day 5 ....

Day 2 .... Day 6 ....

Day 3 .... Day 7 ....

Day 4 ....

B Write the day before: Write the day after:

Tuesday ......Monday......   Wednesday ....

Friday ....   Saturday ....

Sunday ....   Monday ....

Wednesday ....   Thursday ....

Monday ....   Tuesday ....

C Write the first three letters of the day which comes:

2 days before Monday ......Sat......   3 days after Friday ....

4 days after Wednesday ....   5 days before Saturday ....

3 days before Friday ....   4 days after Tuesday ....

5 days after Thursday ....   3 days before Sunday ....

4 days before Tuesday ....   6 days after Monday ....

Sheet 25 COUNTING 2

Fill in the boxes.

A

9 10 11 ☐ ☐	11 count on 4 ☐	14 count back 5 ☐
10 9 8 ☐ ☐	14 count on 5 ☐	11 count back 8 ☐
16 17 18 ☐ ☐	5 count on 7 ☐	17 count back 4 ☐
17 16 15 ☐ ☐	17 count on 3 ☐	13 count back 5 ☐
15 16 17 ☐ ☐	12 count on 6 ☐	20 count back 6 ☐

0 1 2 3 4 5 6 7 8 9 10 11 12 13 14 15 16 17 18 19 20

B

Count on — Count back

48 47 46 ☐ ☐	4 from 98 ☐	5 from 61 ☐
97 98 99 ☐ ☐	6 from 47 ☐	4 from 103 ☐
72 71 70 ☐ ☐	7 from 85 ☐	6 from 35 ☐
26 27 28 ☐ ☐	5 from 59 ☐	4 from 82 ☐
103 102 101 ☐ ☐	6 from 95 ☐	7 from 105 ☐

0 10 20 30 40 50 60 70 80 90 100

C

Count on — Count back

133 132 131 ☐ ☐	6 from 125 ☐	4 from 120 ☐
116 117 118 ☐ ☐	8 from 164 ☐	7 from 154 ☐
182 181 180 ☐ ☐	5 from 108 ☐	6 from 101 ☐
97 98 99 ☐ ☐	7 from 185 ☐	8 from 142 ☐
202 201 200 ☐ ☐	6 from 99 ☐	7 from 163 ☐

Sheet 26 READING AND WRITING NUMBERS 2

A

Write in figures.

eleven — 11

twelve —

thirteen —

fourteen —

fifteen —

sixteen —

seventeen —

eighteen —

nineteen —

twenty —

Write in words.

6 — six

2 — ....

9 — ....

5 — ....

8 — ....

1 — ....

4 — ....

7 — ....

3 — ....

B

Write in figures.

ten —

twenty —

thirty —

forty —

fifty —

sixty —

seventy —

eighty —

ninety —

one hundred —

Write in words.

18 — ....

13 — ....

16 — ....

14 — ....

19 — ....

12 — ....

17 — ....

15 — ....

11 — ....

C

Write in figures.

twenty-three —

seventy-nine —

forty-six —

ninety-one —

thirty-five —

sixty-eight —

eighty-two —

fifty-four —

twenty-seven —

ninety-nine —

Write in words.

75 — ....

33 — ....

97 — ....

28 — ....

64 — ....

41 — ....

89 — ....

52 — ....

76 — ....

Sheet 27 USING NUMBER LINES

Write the numbers in the boxes.

A

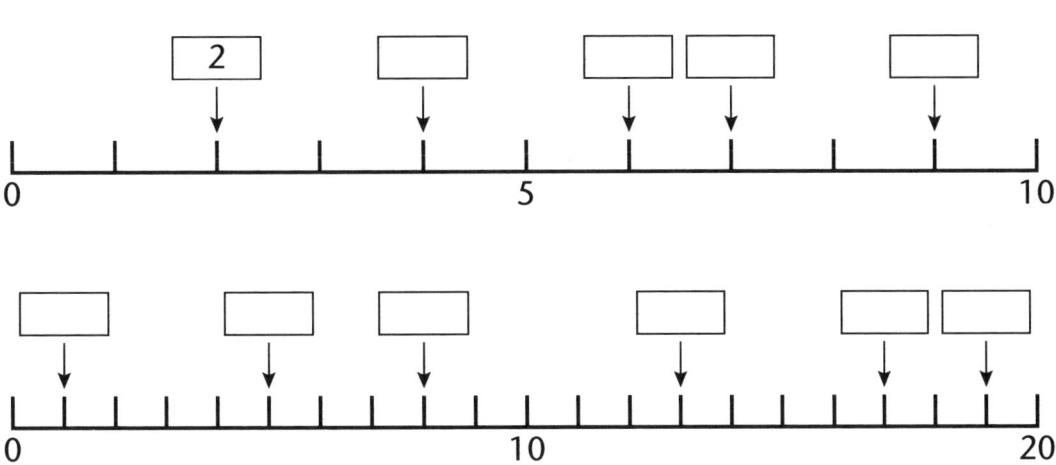

B

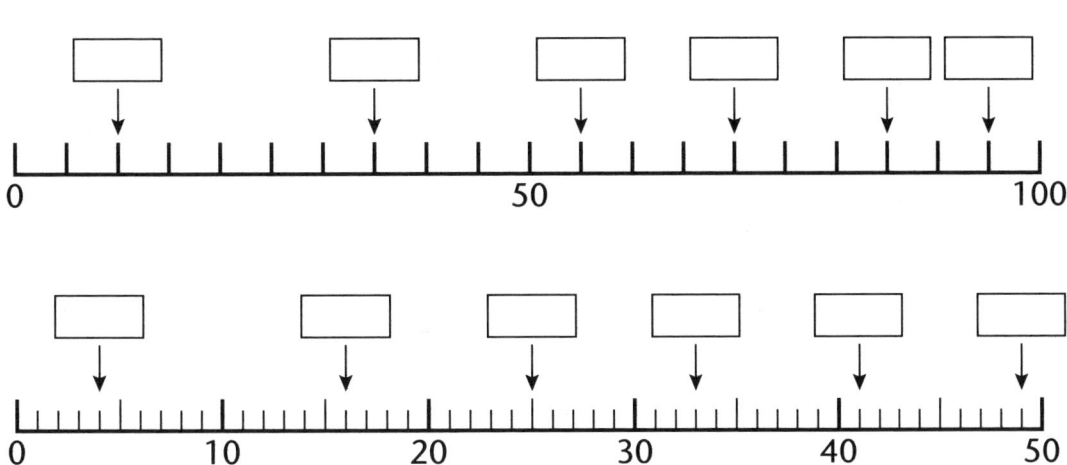

C

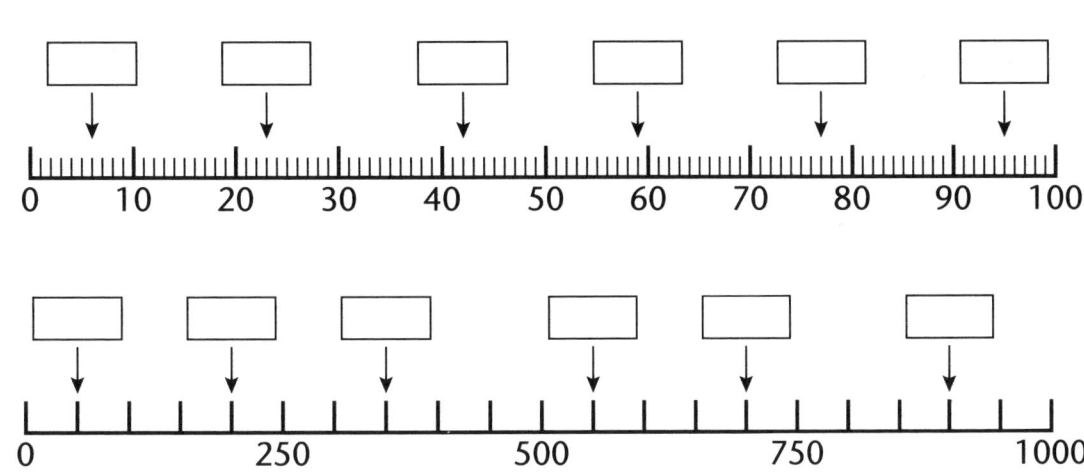

Sheet 28 ADDITION FACTS 2

Fill in the boxes.

A

3 + 2 = 5   6 + 4 = ☐   7 + 3 = ☐   3 + 7 = ☐

5 + 4 = ☐   1 + 8 = ☐   2 + 4 = ☐   6 + 3 = ☐

0 + 8 = ☐   0 + 7 = ☐   5 + 5 = ☐   2 + 6 = ☐

7 + 1 = ☐   5 + 2 = ☐   4 + 3 = ☐   1 + 4 = ☐

4 + 2 = ☐   3 + 5 = ☐   9 + 1 = ☐   8 + 2 = ☐

B

8 + 5 = ☐   12 + 6 = ☐   3 + 9 = ☐   15 + 3 = ☐

13 + 7 = ☐   6 + 7 = ☐   7 + 8 = ☐   4 + 13 = ☐

9 + 6 = ☐   8 + 11 = ☐   6 + 14 = ☐   7 + 5 = ☐

5 + 12 = ☐   14 + 3 = ☐   9 + 7 = ☐   8 + 9 = ☐

7 + 4 = ☐   9 + 9 = ☐   11 + 8 = ☐   6 + 8 = ☐

C

27 + 6 = ☐   49 + 9 = ☐   87 + 4 = ☐   78 + 7 = ☐

59 + 7 = ☐   84 + 7 = ☐   56 + 8 = ☐   53 + 9 = ☐

83 + 8 = ☐   37 + 8 = ☐   42 + 9 = ☐   45 + 8 = ☐

65 + 7 = ☐   26 + 5 = ☐   28 + 3 = ☐   89 + 5 = ☐

76 + 9 = ☐   68 + 8 = ☐   34 + 9 = ☐   67 + 7 = ☐

Sheet 29 ADDITION PROBLEMS 2

Fill in the boxes.

A

Add 4 to 4 ☐   3 add 7 ☐   6 and 3 make ☐
Add 6 to 1 ☐   1 add 4 ☐   1 and 9 make ☐
Add 2 to 3 ☐   7 add 2 ☐   5 and 3 make ☐
Add 5 to 0 ☐   2 add 5 ☐   10 and 0 make ☐
Add 8 to 2 ☐   4 add 6 ☐   3 and 4 make ☐

B

7 and 9 is ☐ altogether.   9 and 5 equals ☐
The sum of 4 and 8 is ☐.   6 and 14 equals ☐
How many is 12 and 6 altogether? ☐   15 and 2 equals ☐
5 added to 15 makes ☐.   11 and 9 equals ☐
The total of 14 and 0 is ☐.   8 and 8 equals ☐
☐ is 3 more than 12   13 and 6 equals ☐

C

☐ added to 12 equals 20.   ☐ add 5 is 14
7 is ☐ more than 11.   17 add ☐ is 20
☐ and 9 have a sum of 15.   ☐ add 8 is 17
The total of 10 and ☐ is 50.   70 add ☐ is 100
☐ plus 0 equals 12.   ☐ add 5 is 13
Altogether ☐ and 6 makes 19   ☐ add 12 is 16

Sheet 30 MAKING TOTALS 1

Fill in the boxes.

A

Make 6
4 + 2
1 +
0 +
3 +

Make 10
9 +
2 +
7 +
5 +

Make 8
4 +
8 +
3 +
6 +

Make 10
4 +
0 +
3 +
8 +

B

Make 12
5 +
8 +
6 +
9 +

Make 20
6 +
11 +
3 +
15 +

Make 15
7 +
12 +
0 +
9 +

Make 20
8 +
13 +
4 +
20 +

C

Make 24
8 +
14 +
6 +
17 +

Make 100
20 +
70 +
50 +
100 +

Make 50
35 +
43 +
25 +
39 +

Make 100
60 +
10 +
100 +
30 +

Sheet 31   COMPARING WEIGHTS

A

Colour the pictures.   light → yellow   heavy → red

B

Colour the pictures.   light → yellow   heavier → green   heaviest → red

C

Fill in the boxes.

Mum   60 kg
Dad   80 kg

Mum is ☐ kg lighter.

butter   200 g
cheese   300 g

The cheese is ☐ g heavier.

rubber   20 g
pencil   2 g

The pencil is ☐ g lighter.

Harry   23 kg
Tim   18 kg

Harry is ☐ kg heavier.

Sheet 32   MEASURING WEIGHT 1

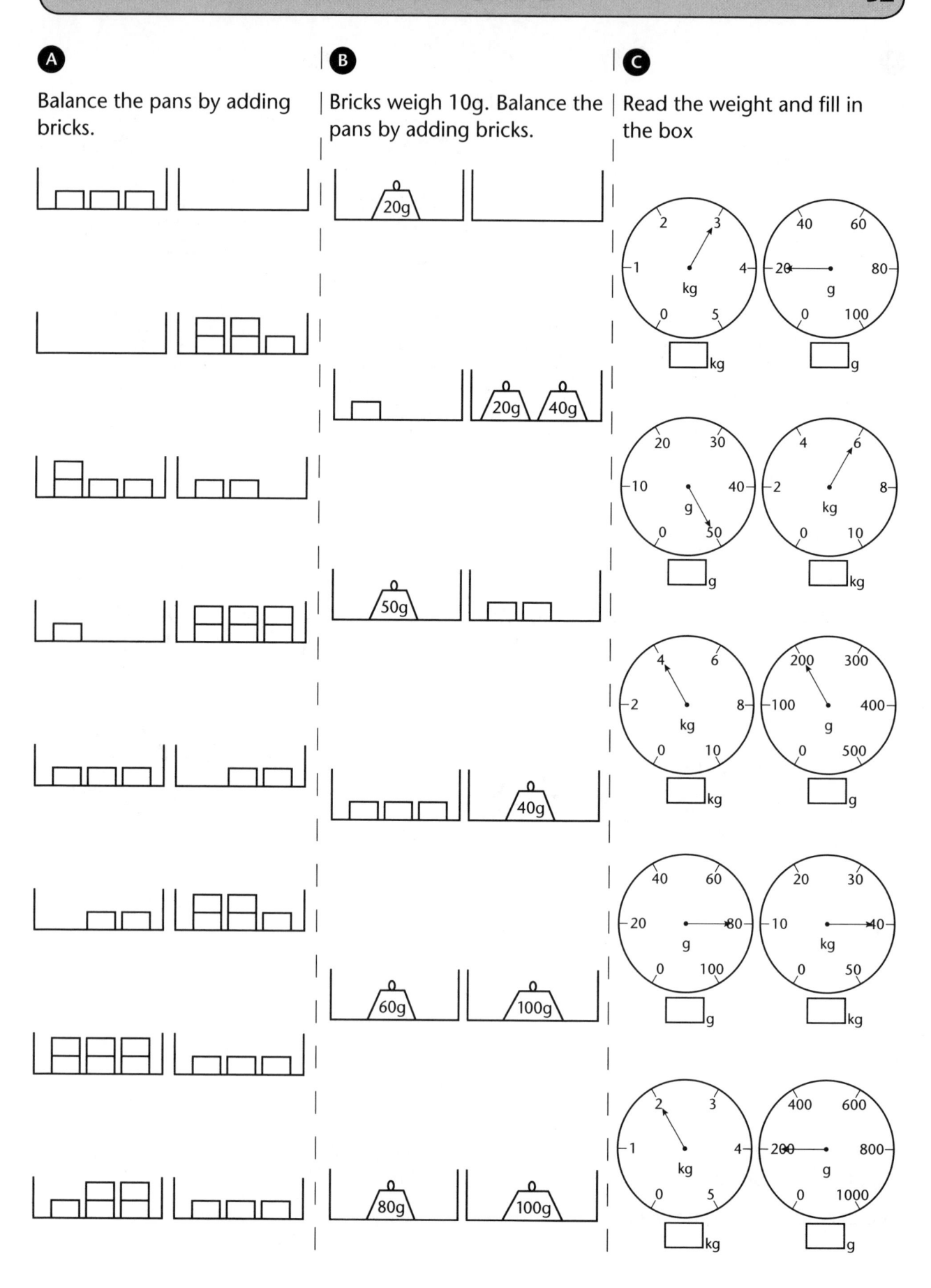

A
Balance the pans by adding bricks.

B
Bricks weigh 10g. Balance the pans by adding bricks.

C
Read the weight and fill in the box

Sheet 33 MEASURING WEIGHT 2

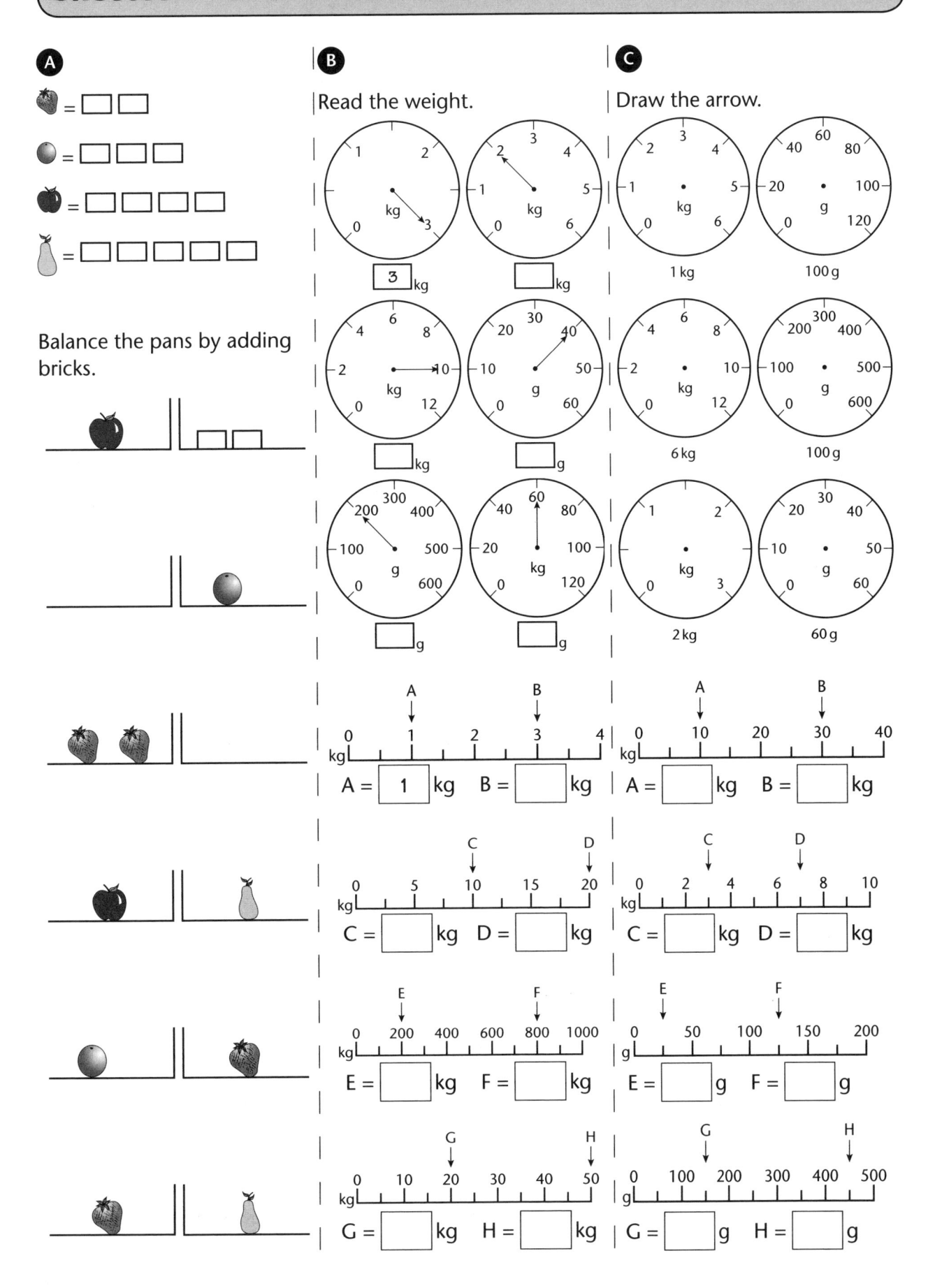

A

🍓 = ☐☐
🍊 = ☐☐☐
🍎 = ☐☐☐☐
🍐 = ☐☐☐☐☐

Balance the pans by adding bricks.

B

Read the weight.

3	kg
☐	kg
☐	kg
☐	g
☐	g
☐	g

A = 1 kg   B = ☐ kg

C = ☐ kg   D = ☐ kg

E = ☐ kg   F = ☐ kg

G = ☐ kg   H = ☐ kg

C

Draw the arrow.

1 kg   100 g
6 kg   100 g
2 kg   60 g

A = ☐ kg   B = ☐ kg

C = ☐ kg   D = ☐ kg

E = ☐ g   F = ☐ g

G = ☐ g   H = ☐ g

Sheet 34   COUNTING IN FIVES

A

Write the numbers.

five ☐   thirty ☐
ten ☐   thirty-five ☐
fifteen ☐   forty ☐
twenty ☐   forty-five ☐
twenty-five ☐   fifty ☐

Write the words.

5 ..five..   30 ....
10 ....   35 ....
15 ....   40 ....
20 ....   45 ....
25 ....   50 ....

B

Fill in the boxes.

15 20 25 ☐ ☐
0   5   10 ☐ ☐
40 45 50 ☐ ☐
10 15 20 ☐ ☐
25 30 35 ☐ ☐

Count on.

4 fives from 40 ☐
6 fives from 5 ☐
3 fives from 35 ☐
5 fives from 10 ☐
4 fives from 25 ☐

Count on.

2 fives from 50 ☐
7 fives from 0 ☐
5 fives from 15 ☐
3 fives from 40 ☐
6 fives from 20 ☐

C

Fill in the boxes.

58 63 68 ☐ ☐
42 47 52 ☐ ☐
79 84 89 ☐ ☐
21 26 31 ☐ ☐
87 92 97 ☐ ☐

Count on.

4 fives from 42 ☐
5 fives from 96 ☐
6 fives from 17 ☐
3 fives from 84 ☐
7 fives from 38 ☐

Count on.

6 fives from 61 ☐
3 fives from 29 ☐
4 fives from 52 ☐
8 fives from 46 ☐
6 fives from 74 ☐

Sheet 35 COUNTING IN TENS

A

Write the numbers.

ten	10	sixty		
twenty		seventy		
thirty		eighty		
forty		ninety		
fifty		one hundred		

Write the words.

10 ....   60 ....
20 ....   70 ....
30 ....   80 ....
40 ....   90 ....
50 ....   100 ....

B

Fill in the boxes.

0 10 20 ☐ ☐
40 50 60 ☐ ☐
60 70 80 ☐ ☐
20 30 40 ☐ ☐
50 60 70 ☐ ☐

Count on.

3 tens from 60 ☐
6 tens from 0 ☐
4 tens from 30 ☐
5 tens from 50 ☐
3 tens from 20 ☐

Count on.

2 tens from 80 ☐
7 tens from 10 ☐
3 tens from 60 ☐
5 tens from 20 ☐
6 tens from 40 ☐

C

Fill in the boxes.

23 33 43 ☐ ☐
67 77 87 ☐ ☐
59 69 79 ☐ ☐
31 41 51 ☐ ☐
75 85 95 ☐ ☐

Count on.

4 tens from 42 ☐
5 tens from 96 ☐
6 tens from 17 ☐
3 tens from 84 ☐
7 tens from 38 ☐

Count on.

6 tens from 61 ☐
3 tens from 29 ☐
4 tens from 52 ☐
8 tens from 46 ☐
6 tens from 74 ☐

Sheet 36   SUBTRACTION FACTS 2

Fill in the boxes.

A

8 − 3 = 5   6 − 0 = ☐   7 − 5 = ☐   10 − 5 = ☐

10 − 6 = ☐   4 − 3 = ☐   10 − 4 = ☐   7 − 3 = ☐

7 − 2 = ☐   10 − 2 = ☐   6 − 4 = ☐   8 − 4 = ☐

5 − 4 = ☐   9 − 4 = ☐   5 − 2 = ☐   3 − 3 = ☐

9 − 7 = ☐   8 − 7 = ☐   9 − 8 = ☐   9 − 2 = ☐

B

15 − 6 = ☐   20 − 13 = ☐   19 − 15 = ☐   18 − 9 = ☐

13 − 8 = ☐   16 − 8 = ☐   11 − 9 = ☐   20 − 6 = ☐

19 − 7 = ☐   14 − 9 = ☐   17 − 6 = ☐   12 − 3 = ☐

11 − 4 = ☐   18 − 5 = ☐   15 − 8 = ☐   16 − 5 = ☐

17 − 9 = ☐   12 − 6 = ☐   13 − 4 = ☐   14 − 7 = ☐

C

23 − 7 = ☐   67 − 8 = ☐   58 − 9 = ☐   96 − 7 = ☐

80 − 2 = ☐   94 − 6 = ☐   25 − 7 = ☐   22 − 5 = ☐

46 − 9 = ☐   50 − 5 = ☐   43 − 6 = ☐   57 − 9 = ☐

51 − 6 = ☐   39 − 0 = ☐   30 − 3 = ☐   64 − 8 = ☐

35 − 8 = ☐   82 − 6 = ☐   71 − 8 = ☐   100 − 6 = ☐

Sheet 37 SUBTRACTION PROBLEMS 2

Fill in the boxes.

A

9 take 5 ☐   Take 4 from 10 ☐   8 take 5 ☐
6 take 2 ☐   Take 0 from 8 ☐   9 take 3 ☐
8 take 4 ☐   Take 5 from 7 ☐   5 take 5 ☐
10 take 3 ☐   Take 7 from 9 ☐   10 take 2 ☐
7 take 2 ☐   Take 1 from 6 ☐   7 take 3 ☐
9 take 1 ☐   Take 9 from 10 ☐   8 take 1 ☐

B

What is 9 less than 17? ☐
16 take 3 is ☐ .
The difference between 15 and 20 is ☐ .
Take away 7 from 16. ☐
Find the difference between 13 and 6. ☐
5 less than 11 is ☐ .

15 fewer than 19 ☐
4 fewer than 12 ☐
13 fewer than 18 ☐
9 fewer than 15 ☐
8 fewer than 20 ☐
7 fewer than 14 ☐

C

Take 8 from 26. ☐
How many is 5 less than 54? ☐
Subtract 10 from 100. ☐
What is the difference between 7 and 83? ☐
Find 65 minus 10. ☐
How many is 90 take 30. ☐

31 subtract 9 ☐
70 subtract 40 ☐
43 subtract 5 ☐
100 subtract 50 ☐
96 subtract 7 ☐
50 subtract 44 ☐

Sheet 38 MISSING NUMBER PROBLEMS 1

Fill in the boxes.

A

2 + [6] = 8   [10] − 5 = 5   9 − [ ] = 5

6 + [ ] = 10   [ ] − 6 = 0   8 − [ ] = 7

4 + [ ] = 7   [ ] − 7 = 2   5 − [ ] = 0

3 + [ ] = 9   [ ] − 5 = 3   10 − [ ] = 3

4 + [ ] = 6   [ ] − 1 = 9   7 − [ ] = 2

B

8 + [ ] = 14   [ ] − 6 = 13   16 − [ ] = 4

6 + [ ] = 18   [ ] − 5 = 9   13 − [ ] = 7

11 + [ ] = 20   [ ] − 7 = 13   17 − [ ] = 8

7 + [ ] = 15   [ ] − 6 = 6   20 − [ ] = 5

3 + [ ] = 12   [ ] − 13 = 5   11 − [ ] = 3

C

17 + [ ] = 25   [ ] − 60 = 40   53 − [ ] = 9

6 + [ ] = 34   [ ] − 55 = 7   70 − [ ] = 20

50 + [ ] = 80   [ ] − 7 = 76   41 − [ ] = 38

57 + [ ] = 67   [ ] − 10 = 40   96 − [ ] = 80

30 + [ ] = 100   [ ] − 6 = 38   27 − [ ] = 8

Sheet 39 RECOGNISING COINS

A

Write the amounts.

5p + 1p = ☐ p   2p + 1p = ☐ p   10p + 1p = ☐ p

10p + 2p = ☐ p   10p + 5p = ☐ p   5p + 2p = ☐ p

5p + 5p = ☐ p   2p + 2p = ☐ p   10p + 10p = ☐ p

B

Write the amounts.

50p + 10p = ☐ p   20p + 1p = ☐ p   £1 + £1 = £ ☐

20p + 5p = ☐ p   50p + 5p = ☐ p   £2 + £1 = £ ☐

50p + 2p = ☐ p   20p + 10p = ☐ p   £2 + £2 = £ ☐

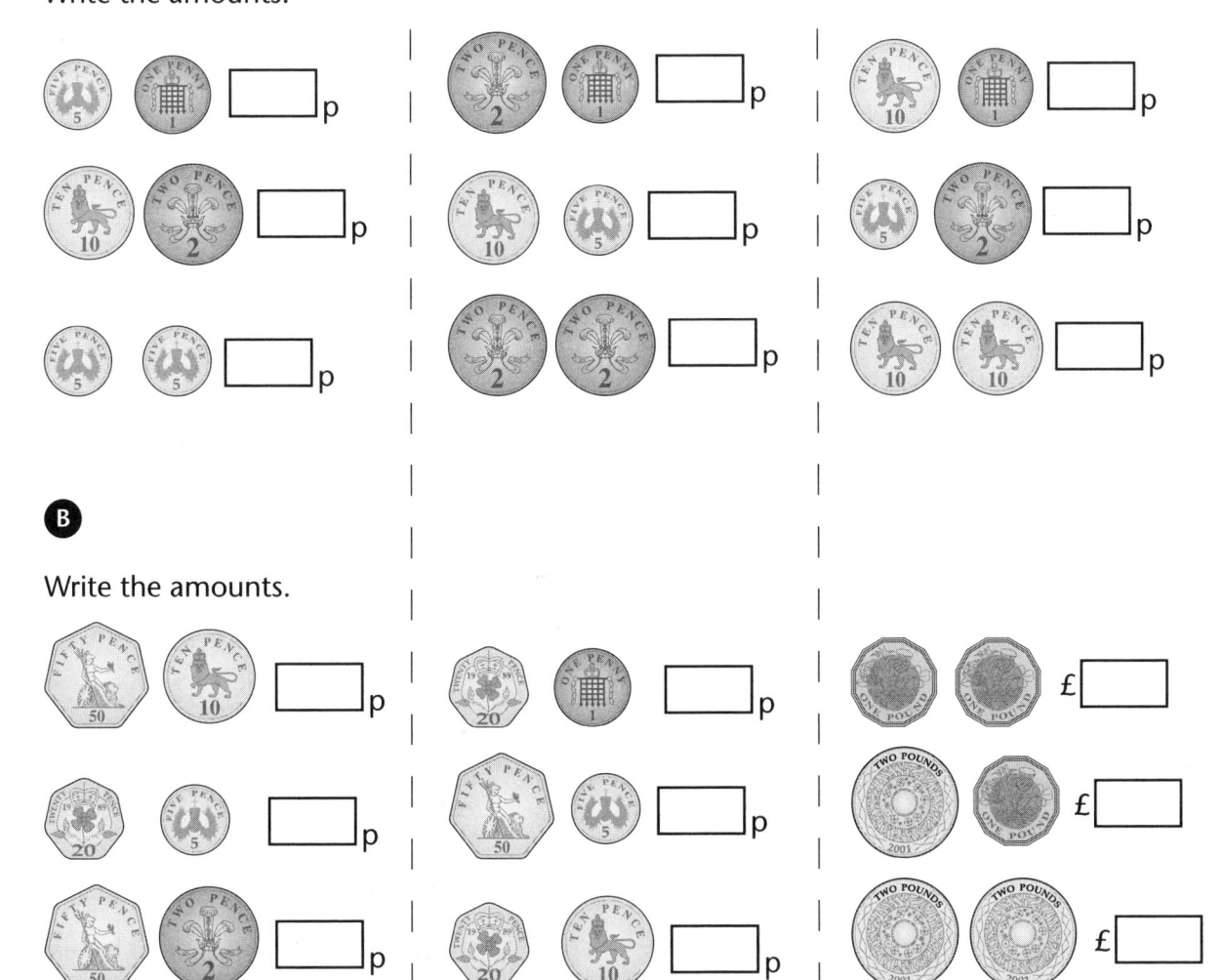

C

Make these amounts. Use the number of coins shown.

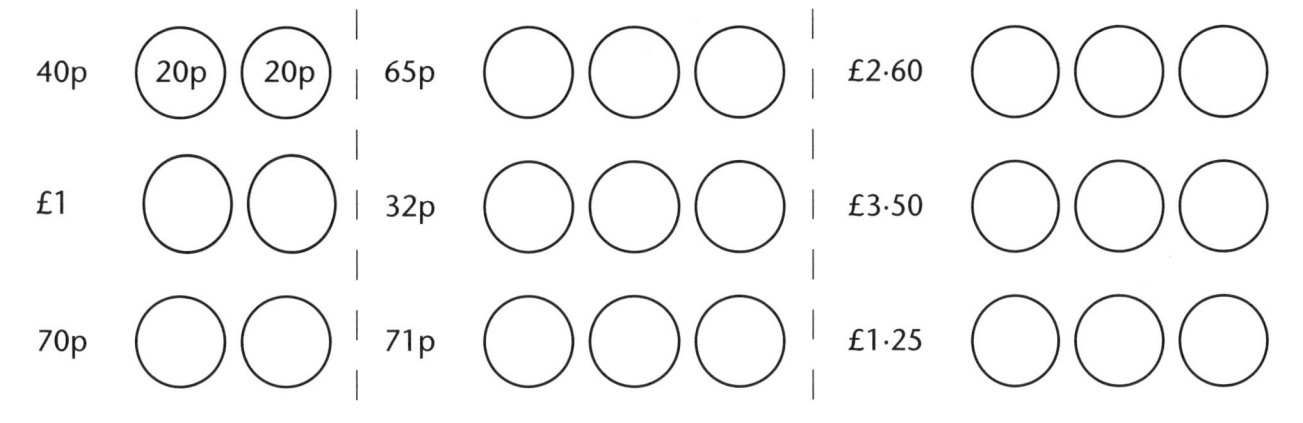

40p (20p)(20p)   65p ◯◯◯   £2·60 ◯◯◯

£1   ◯◯   32p ◯◯◯   £3·50 ◯◯◯

70p ◯◯   71p ◯◯◯   £1·25 ◯◯◯

Sheet 40   3-D SHAPES   40

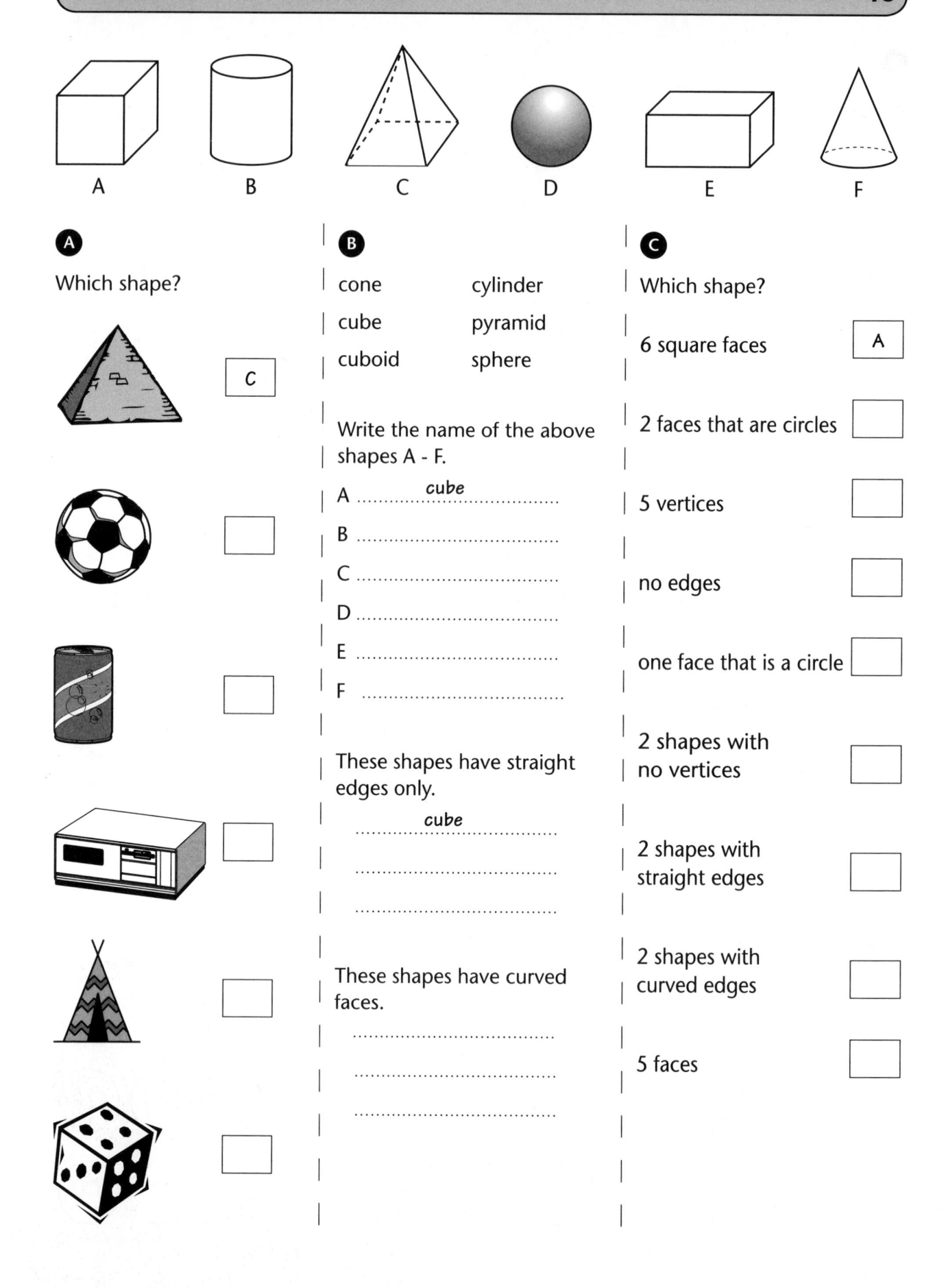

A   B   C   D   E   F

A
Which shape?

- pyramid → C
- football (sphere) → ☐
- can (cylinder) → ☐
- video recorder (cuboid) → ☐
- tepee (cone) → ☐
- dice (cube) → ☐

B
cone   cylinder
cube   pyramid
cuboid   sphere

Write the name of the above shapes A - F.

A ..... cube .....
B ....
C ....
D ....
E ....
F ....

These shapes have straight edges only.

..... cube .....
....
....

These shapes have curved faces.

....
....
....

C
Which shape?

6 square faces → A

2 faces that are circles → ☐

5 vertices → ☐

no edges → ☐

one face that is a circle → ☐

2 shapes with no vertices → ☐

2 shapes with straight edges → ☐

2 shapes with curved edges → ☐

5 faces → ☐

Sheet 41   DESCRIBING 3-D SHAPES

A

Colour the shapes of the dog and the robot.

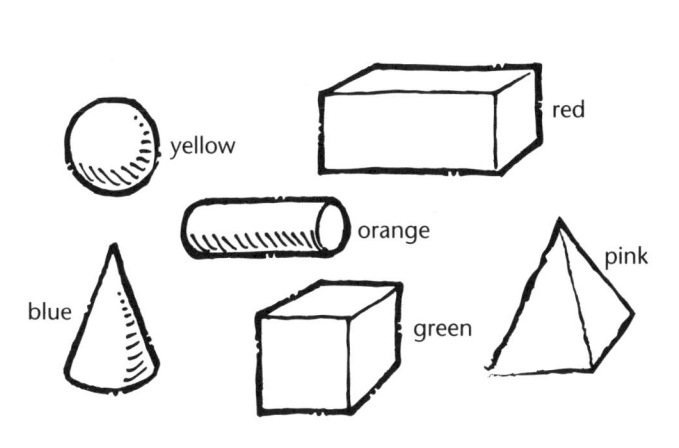

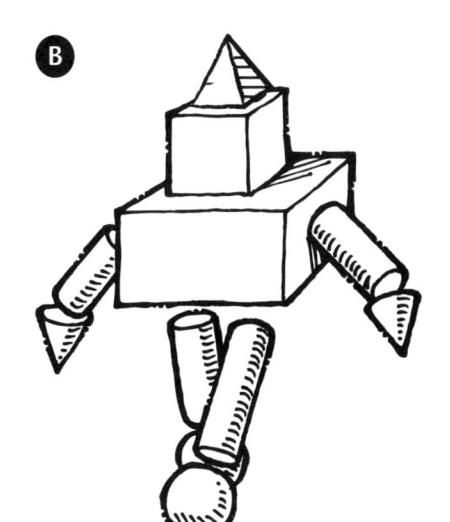

- yellow
- red
- orange
- pink
- blue
- green

B

Complete the table.

Shape	Dog	Robot
spheres	2	
cubes	2	
cones		
cuboids		
cylinders		
pyramids		

C   Match the flat faces of the 3-D shapes with these 2-D shapes.

circle   rectangle   square   triangle

cube ....6 squares........   cuboid ....

cone ....   pyramid ....

cylinder ....

Sheet 42 ARRAYS 2

Use the array to help fill in the boxes.

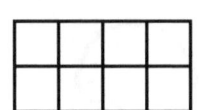

A

2 + 2 + 2 + 2 = [8]

4 lots of 2 =

3 + 3 + 3 =

3 lots of 3 =

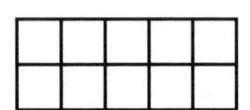

5 + 5 =

2 lots of 5 =

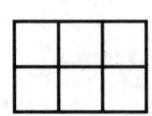

3 lots of 2 =

2 lots of 3 =

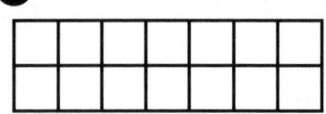

B

7 twos =

2 sevens =

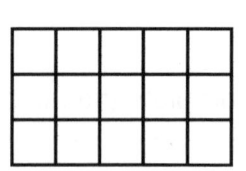

3 fives =

5 threes =

2 sixes =

6 twos =

4 threes =

3 fours =

C

Work out.

4 lots of 5 =

3 lots of 10 =

5 lots of 2 =

6 lots of 5 =

8 tens =

9 twos =

10 fives =

6 tens =

8 × 2 = [16]

7 × 5 =

10 × 10 =

6 × 2 =

5 × 5 =

7 × 10 =

10 × 2 =

9 × 5 =

Sheet 43 GROUPING 2

Draw the groups of dots. Fill in the boxes.

A

How many groups of 2 make 6?

[3] groups of 2 make 6.

How many groups of 4 make 8?

[ ] groups of 4 make 8.

How many groups of 3 make 9?

[ ] groups of 3 make 9.

How many groups of 2 make 12?

[ ] groups of 2 make 12.

B

How many groups of 4 make 12?

[ ] groups of 4 make 12.

How many groups of 3 make 15?

[ ] groups of 3 make 15.

How many groups of 2 make 14?

[ ] groups of 2 make 14.

How many groups of 5 make 15?

[ ] groups of 5 make 15.

C

How many groups of 6 make 18?

[ ] groups of 6 make 18.

How many groups of 4 make 20?

[ ] groups of 4 make 20.

How many groups of 3 make 21?

[ ] groups of 3 make 21.

How many groups of 2 make 16

[ ] groups of 2 make 16.

Sheet 44   HALVES AND QUARTERS OF LINES   44

A

Label each half of the line. Write $\frac{1}{2}$ at the halfway mark.

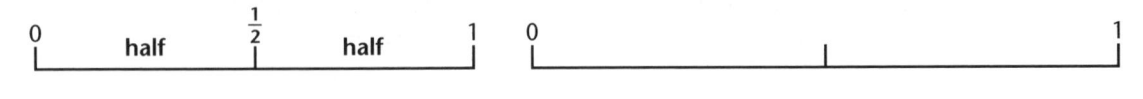

B

Label each quarter by writing qtr. Write $\frac{1}{4}$, $\frac{1}{2}$ or $\frac{3}{4}$ at the marks.

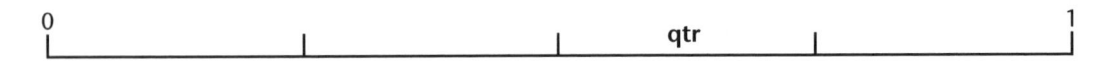

C

Use a ruler. Make marks at each quarter. Label the marks $\frac{1}{4}$, $\frac{1}{2}$ and $\frac{3}{4}$.

Label the marks by writing a fraction.

Sheet 45 HALVES AND QUARTERS OF SHAPES

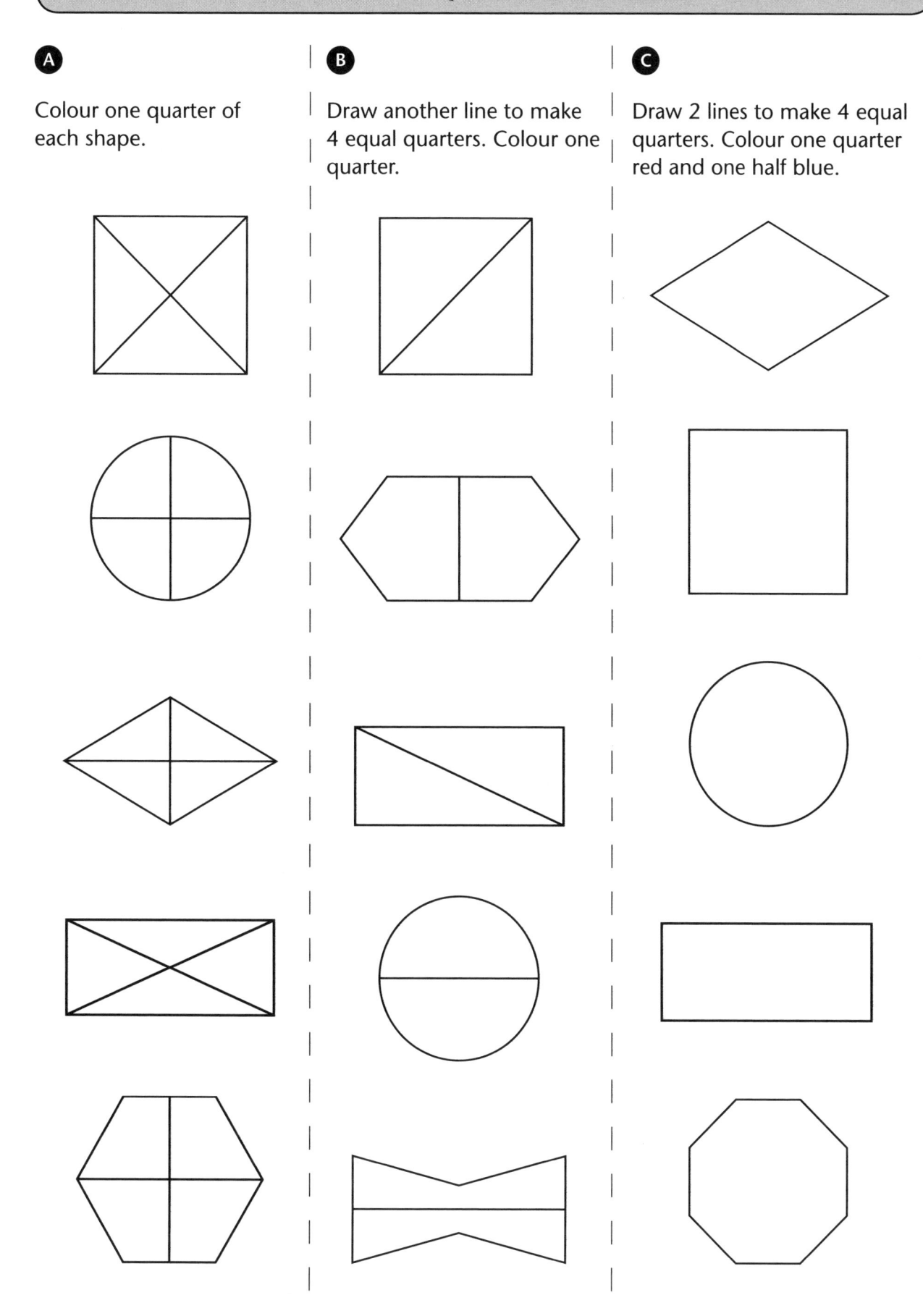

A
Colour one quarter of each shape.

B
Draw another line to make 4 equal quarters. Colour one quarter.

C
Draw 2 lines to make 4 equal quarters. Colour one quarter red and one half blue.

Sheet 46 MAKING TOTALS 2

Fill in the boxes.

A

Make 10
3 + [7]
9 + [ ]
6 + [ ]
2 + [ ]

Make 7
5 + [ ]
1 + [ ]
3 + [ ]
7 + [ ]

Make 10
5 + [ ]
10 + [ ]
7 + [ ]
4 + [ ]

Make 9
4 + [ ]
0 + [ ]
2 + [ ]
6 + [ ]

B

Make 20
17 + [ ]
5 + [ ]
19 + [ ]
14 + [ ]

Make 13
6 + [ ]
0 + [ ]
9 + [ ]
2 + [ ]

Make 20
8 + [ ]
20 + [ ]
4 + [ ]
13 + [ ]

Make 16
7 + [ ]
3 + [ ]
10 + [ ]
8 + [ ]

C

Make 100
30 + [ ]
0 + [ ]
50 + [ ]
90 + [ ]

Make 25
17 + [ ]
20 + [ ]
9 + [ ]
12 + [ ]

Make 100
80 + [ ]
40 + [ ]
70 + [ ]
10 + [ ]

Make 60
20 + [ ]
50 + [ ]
15 + [ ]
35 + [ ]

Sheet 47 +/− PROBLEMS 1

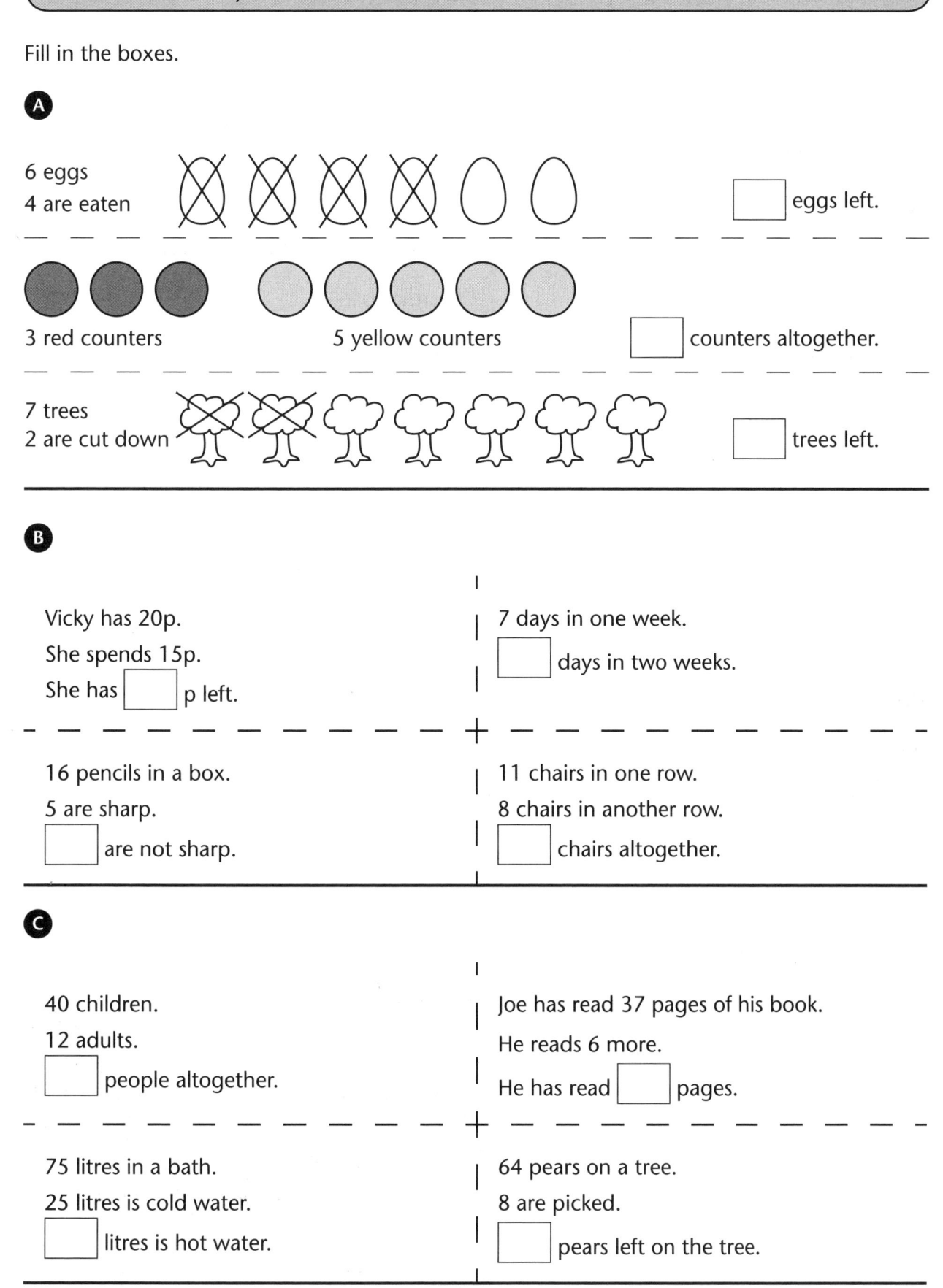

Fill in the boxes.

A

6 eggs
4 are eaten   ☒ ☒ ☒ ☒ ◯ ◯   ☐ eggs left.

3 red counters   5 yellow counters   ☐ counters altogether.

7 trees
2 are cut down   ☐ trees left.

B

Vicky has 20p.
She spends 15p.
She has ☐ p left.

7 days in one week.
☐ days in two weeks.

16 pencils in a box.
5 are sharp.
☐ are not sharp.

11 chairs in one row.
8 chairs in another row.
☐ chairs altogether.

C

40 children.
12 adults.
☐ people altogether.

Joe has read 37 pages of his book.
He reads 6 more.
He has read ☐ pages.

75 litres in a bath.
25 litres is cold water.
☐ litres is hot water.

64 pears on a tree.
8 are picked.
☐ pears left on the tree.

Sheet 48   MONTHS OF THE YEAR

April	February	June	November
August	January	March	October
December	July	May	September

A

This month ....

Last month ....

Next month ....

There are ☐ months in a year

Christmas is in ....

My birthday is in ....

B Use a calendar. Write the months in the correct order.

1. January
2. ....
3. ....
4. ....
5. ....
6. ....
7. ....
8. ....
9. ....
10. ....
11. ....
12. ....

C

	Day	Month	Year
Today's date	....	....	....
The day I was born	....	....	....
First day of next year	....	....	....
Last day of last year	....	....	....
Christmas Day this year	....	....	....

Sheet 49 CLOCKS 1

49

Write the time in the box.

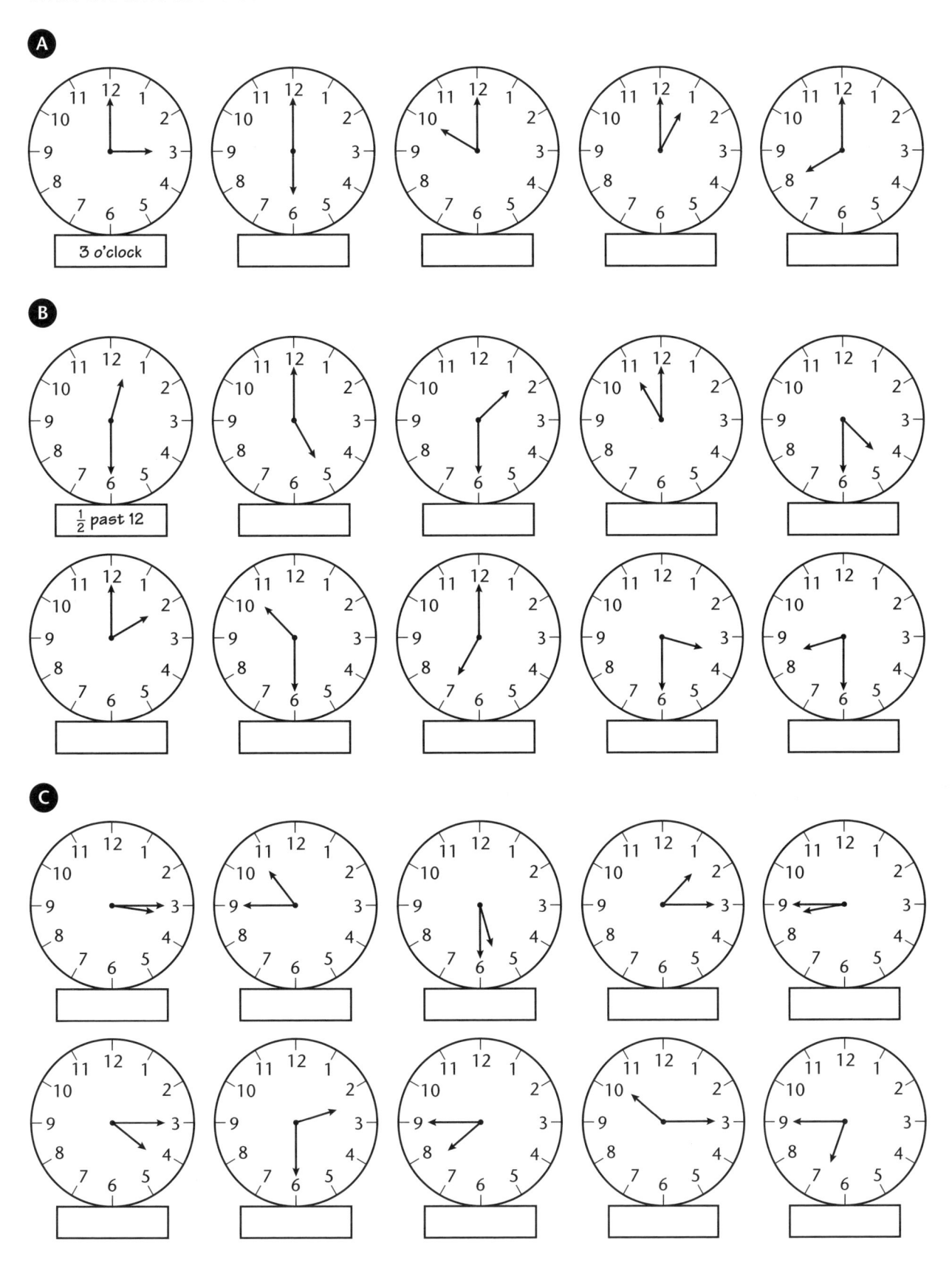

A

3 o'clock

B

½ past 12

C

Sheet 50   FIRST, SECOND, THIRD...

A

Write first, second, third or fourth in each space.

first

fourth

first

B

Write the missing positions.

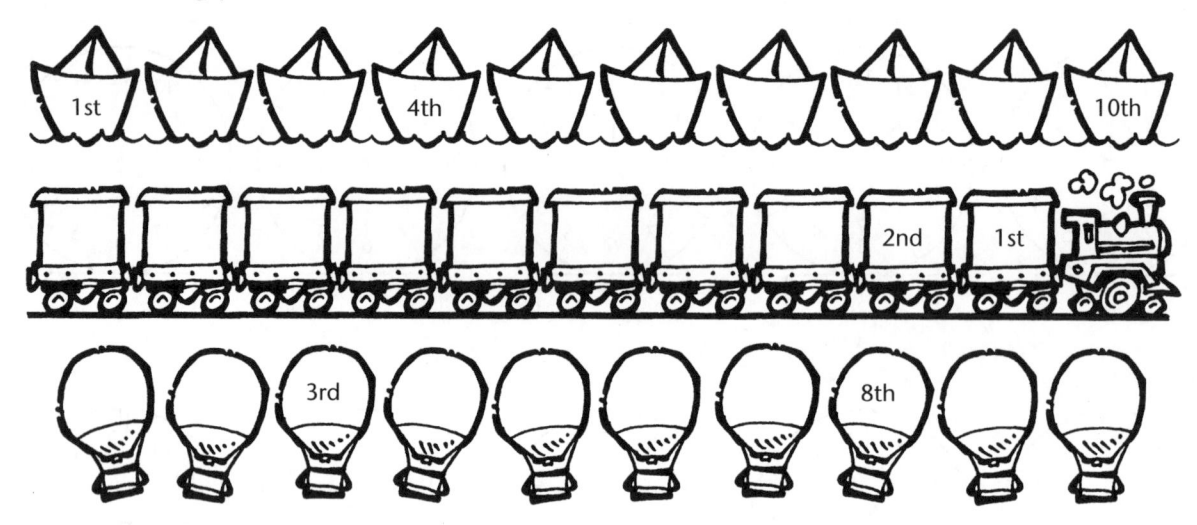

1st ... 4th ... 10th

2nd 1st

3rd ... 8th

C

a b c d e f g h i j k l m n o p

Which letter of the alphabet is:

5th ☐   3rd ☐

9th ☐   12th ☐

14th ☐   6th ☐

7th ☐   15th ☐

○○○○○○○○○○○○

Colour the counters.

blue → fourth, eighth, eleventh

yellow → second, sixth, ninth

red → first, seventh, twelfth

green → third, fifth, tenth

Sheet 51   PLACE VALUE

A

Fill in the boxes.

13 = [10] + 3   19 = [ ] + 9   17 = [ ] + 7

18 = 10 + [ ]   16 = 10 + [ ]   15 = 10 + [ ]

11 = [ ] + 1   21 = [ ] + 1   12 = [ ] + 2

25 = 20 + [ ]   14 = 10 + [ ]   23 = 20 + [ ]

B

Fill in the boxes.

29 = [ ] + 9   78 = 70 + [ ]   81 = [ ] + 1

54 = 50 + [ ]   35 = [ ] + 5   53 = 50 + [ ]

97 = [ ] + 7   82 = 80 + [ ]   74 = [ ] + 4

41 = 40 + [ ]   46 = [ ] + 6   95 = 90 + [ ]

63 = [ ] + 3   69 = 60 + [ ]   58 = [ ] + 8

C

Write the value of the underlined digit.

8<u>7</u> [ ]   7<u>2</u> [ ]   1<u>7</u> [ ]   <u>6</u>3 [ ]

<u>3</u>9 [ ]   9<u>3</u> [ ]   <u>4</u>9 [ ]   5<u>2</u> [ ]

<u>4</u>1 [ ]   <u>5</u>9 [ ]   <u>7</u>8 [ ]   8<u>6</u> [ ]

6<u>8</u> [ ]   3<u>6</u> [ ]   <u>9</u>5 [ ]   <u>3</u>7 [ ]

<u>2</u>5 [ ]   8<u>4</u> [ ]   2<u>1</u> [ ]   <u>9</u>8 [ ]

Sheet 52   +/− FACTS 1

Fill in the boxes.

A

5 + 4 = 9

3 + 7 =

6 + 2 =

2 + 5 =

4 + 6 =

7 + 2 =

0 + 5 =

9 + 1 =

7 − 6 =

9 − 3 =

8 − 5 =

10 − 2 =

5 − 5 =

9 − 8 =

10 − 5 =

6 − 3 =

B

7 + 5 =

9 + 8 =

12 + 7 =

8 + 6 =

6 + 9 =

4 + 7 =

5 + 8 =

13 + 5 =

14 − 5 =

20 − 11 =

17 − 6 =

11 − 5 =

15 − 8 =

12 − 7 =

20 − 4 =

18 − 9 =

C

90 + 40 =

40 + 150 =

70 + 80 =

110 + 60 =

80 + 90 =

130 + 70 =

60 + 70 =

50 + 60 =

150 − 60 =

130 − 50 =

160 − 120 =

200 − 90 =

180 − 130 =

110 − 70 =

170 − 50 =

200 − 140 =

Sheet 53 DICE

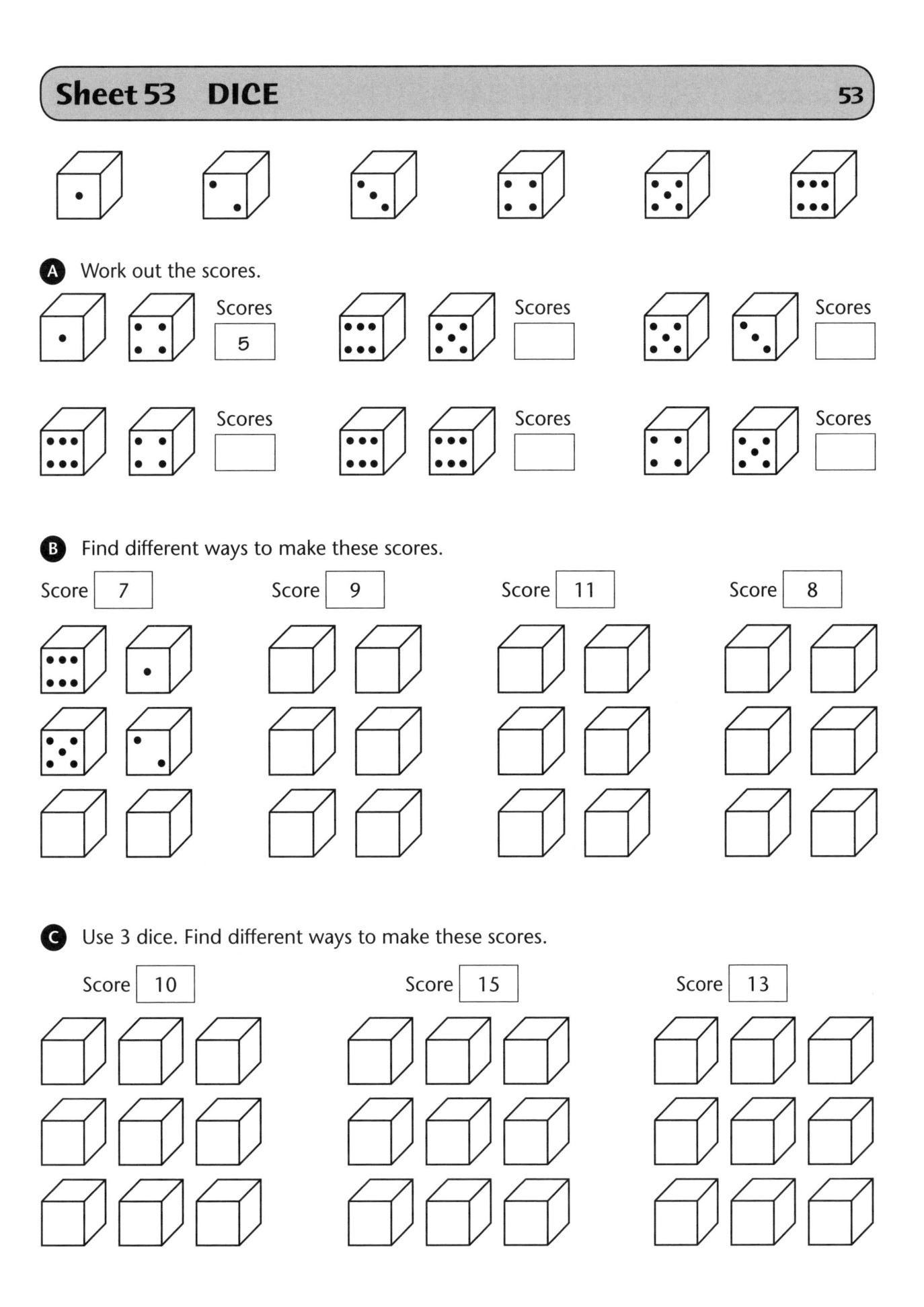

A Work out the scores.

Scores: 5

Scores: ☐

Scores: ☐

Scores: ☐

Scores: ☐

Scores: ☐

B Find different ways to make these scores.

Score 7

Score 9

Score 11

Score 8

C Use 3 dice. Find different ways to make these scores.

Score 10

Score 15

Score 13

Sheet 54   COMPARING CAPACITIES

A

Colour the pictures.   full → blue   nearly empty → yellow

B

Colour the pictures.   full → blue   half full → green   nearly empty → yellow

C

Fill in the boxes.

full bath	100 litres
half full	☐ litres
quarter full	☐ litres

bucket	12 litres
half full	☐ litres
quarter full	☐ litres

full glass	200 ml
half full	☐ ml
quarter full	☐ ml

bottle	1000 ml
half full	☐ ml
quarter full	☐ ml

Sheet 55 MEASURING CAPACITY

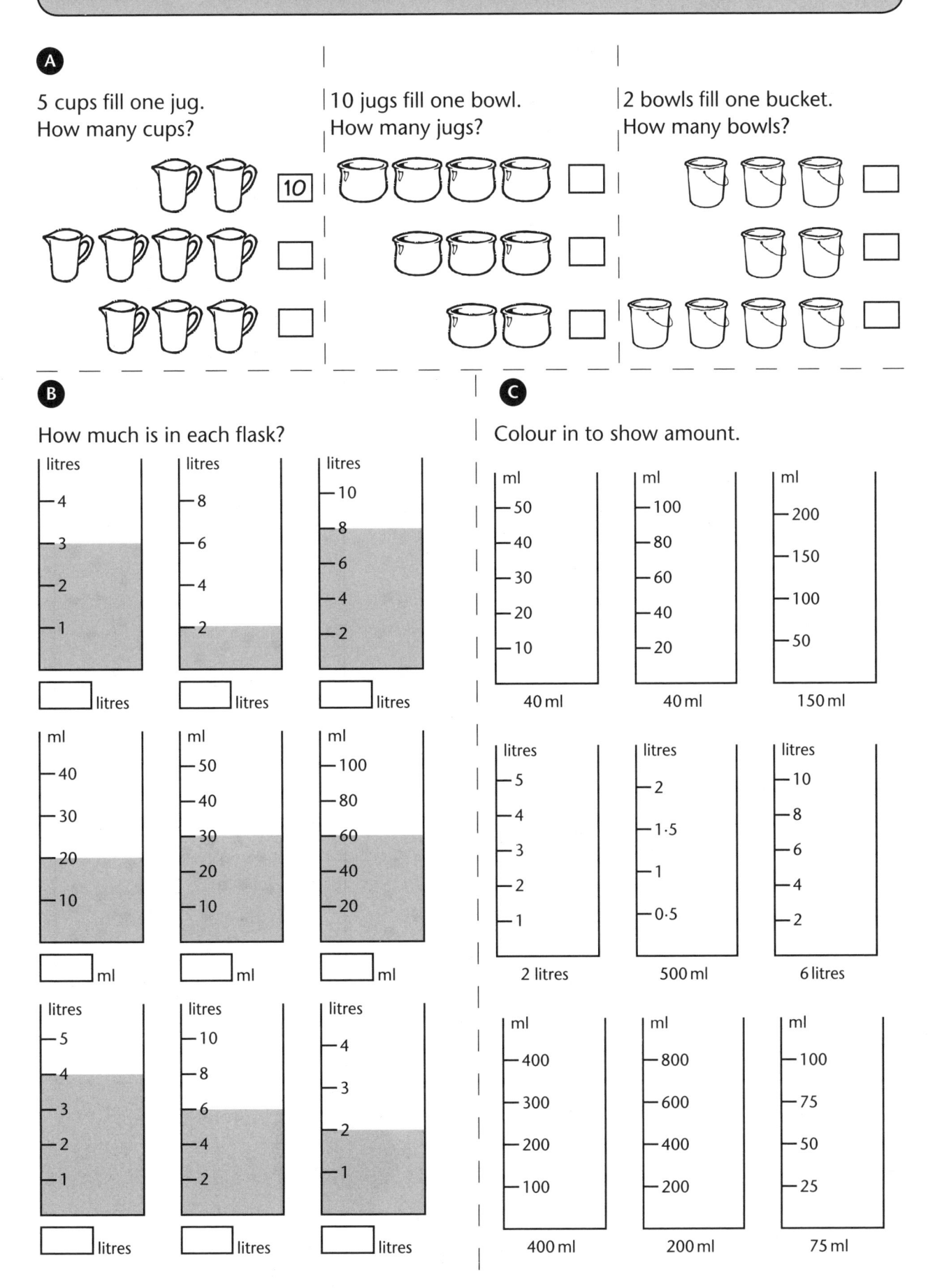

A

5 cups fill one jug.
How many cups?

10 jugs fill one bowl.
How many jugs?

2 bowls fill one bucket.
How many bowls?

B

How much is in each flask?

C

Colour in to show amount.

40 ml   40 ml   150 ml

2 litres   500 ml   6 litres

400 ml   200 ml   75 ml

Sheet 56 COUNTING IN GROUPS

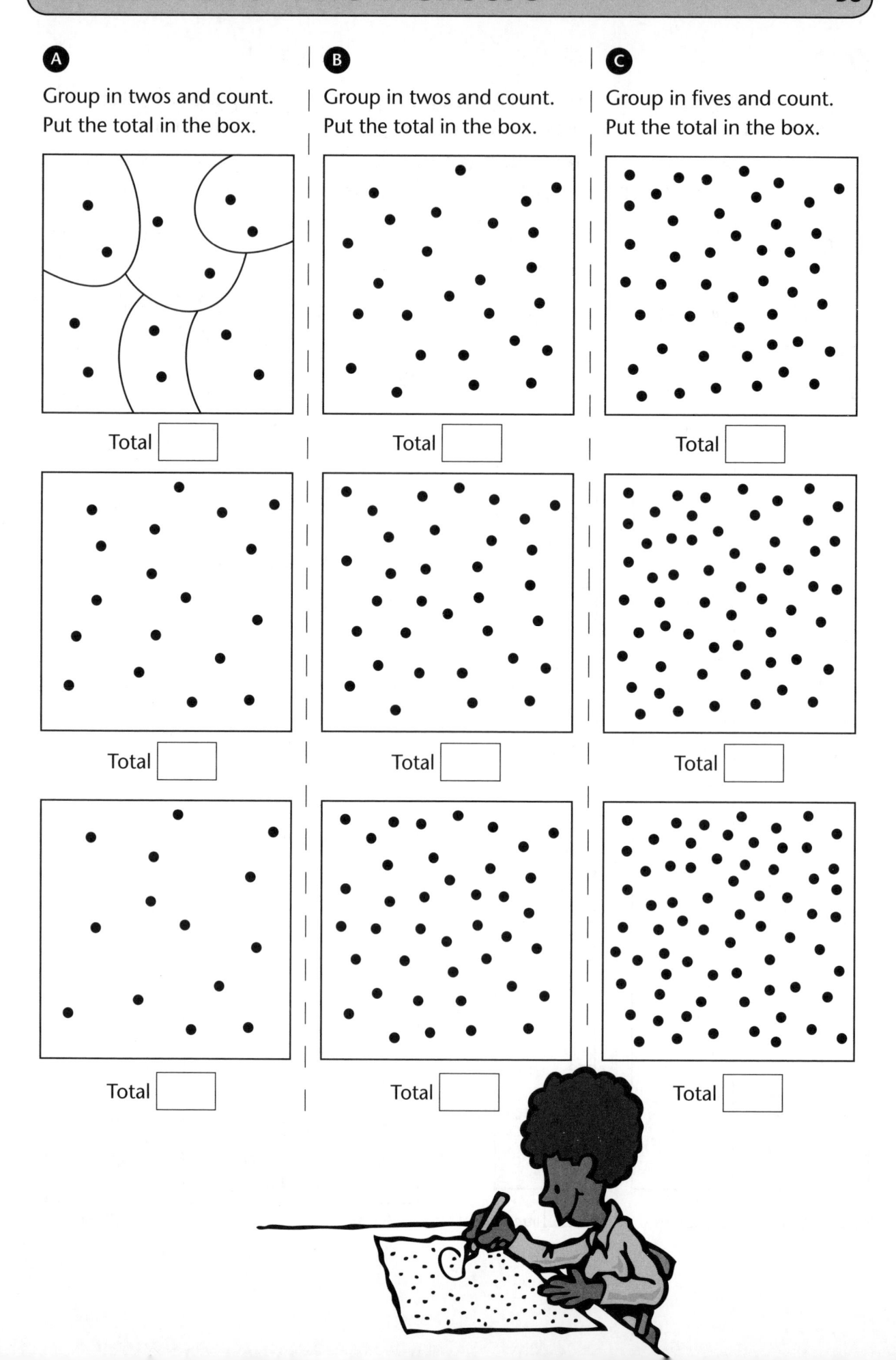

A

Group in twos and count.
Put the total in the box.

Total [ ]

Total [ ]

Total [ ]

B

Group in twos and count.
Put the total in the box.

Total [ ]

Total [ ]

Total [ ]

C

Group in fives and count.
Put the total in the box.

Total [ ]

Total [ ]

Total [ ]

Sheet 57 ODD AND EVEN NUMBERS

A

Fill in the boxes.

Odd	Even
1	2
3	☐
☐	6
7	☐
☐	10
☐	☐
13	☐
☐	☐
☐	18
19	☐

Colour the numbers below:

odd → red   even → blue

1	20
2	19
3	18
4	17
5	16
6	15
7	14
8	13
9	12
10	11

B

Colour the even numbers

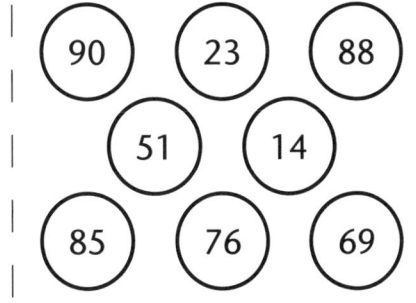

90 23 88
 51 14
85 76 69

Colour the odd numbers

27 72 36
 10 45
91 58 29

Write odd or even.

50 ....

47 ....

83 ....

74 ....

21 ....

38 ....

92 ....

65 ....

C

Colour the numbers:

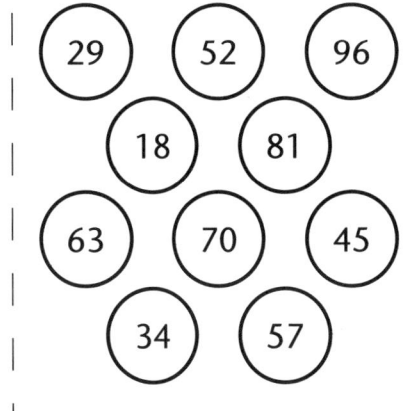

odd → red   even → blue

29 52 96
  18 81
63 70 45
  34 57

Write the 5th even number ☐

Write the 5th odd number ☐

Write odd or even.

186 ....

243 ....

308 ....

419 ....

875 ....

754 ....

667 ....

930 ....

Sheet 58 +/− FACTS 2

Fill in the boxes.

A

4 + 3 = 7
1 + 6 =
8 + 2 =
3 + 6 =

5 + 2 =
10 + 0 =
2 + 7 =
6 + 4 =

8 − 3 =
10 − 9 =
5 − 2 =
7 − 3 =

9 − 5 =
6 − 1 =
10 − 3 =
8 − 6 =

B

6 + 8 =
11 + 7 =
4 + 13 =
9 + 5 =

8 + 3 =
14 + 6 =
7 + 9 =
5 + 8 =

13 − 6 =
16 − 8 =
20 − 12 =
14 − 7 =

19 − 13 =
12 − 9 =
20 − 5 =
16 − 11 =

C

80 + 50 =
90 + 70 =
120 + 80 =
70 + 60 =

50 + 90 =
130 + 40 =
60 + 50 =
90 + 40 =

120 − 70 =
200 − 60 =
140 − 80 =
190 − 50 =

130 − 40 =
200 − 130 =
160 − 50 =
150 − 80 =

Sheet 59   FINDING DIFFERENCES

A

Colour in the smaller number to find the difference.

4 and 1 = 3

5 and 3 = ☐

6 and 2 = ☐

4 and 3 = ☐

5 and 2 = ☐

6 and 4 = ☐

B

Find the difference between each pair of numbers.

10 and 6 = 4

13 and 7 = ☐

11 and 4 = ☐

14 and 5 = ☐

16 and 8 = ☐

19 and 7 = ☐

9 and 2 = ☐

20 and 15 = ☐

12 and 4 = ☐

12 and 9 = ☐

17 and 8 = ☐

20 and 3 = ☐

18 and 10 = ☐

8 and 12 = ☐

14 and 7 = ☐

C

Find the difference between each pair of numbers.

32 and 28 = ☐

46 and 39 = ☐

71 and 63 = ☐

70 and 40 = ☐

80 and 30 = ☐

90 and 20 = ☐

85 and 7 = ☐

53 and 44 = ☐

64 and 48 = ☐

100 and 50 = ☐

100 and 109 = ☐

100 and 80 = ☐

65 and 35 = ☐

97 and 47 = ☐

81 and 51 = ☐

Sheet 60 RECOGNISING NOTES AND COINS

A

Write the amounts.

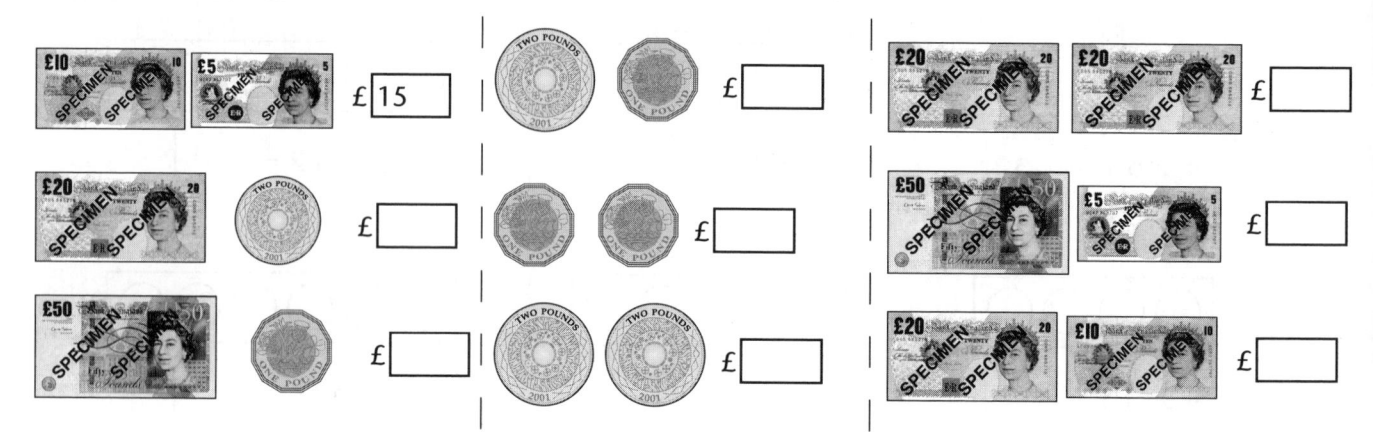

£10 + £5 → £ 15   £2 + £1 → £ ☐   £20 + £20 → £ ☐

£20 + £2 → £ ☐   £1 + £1 → £ ☐   £50 + £5 → £ ☐

£50 + £1 → £ ☐   £2 + £2 → £ ☐   £20 + £10 → £ ☐

B

Write the amounts.

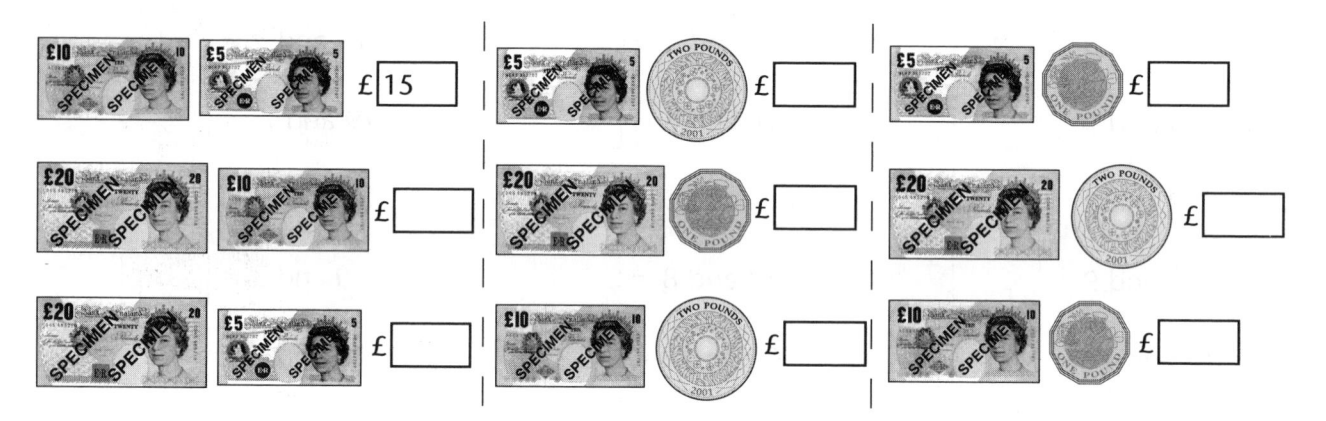

£10 + £5 → £ 15   £5 + £2 → £ ☐   £5 + £1 → £ ☐

£20 + £10 → £ ☐   £20 + £1 → £ ☐   £20 + £2 → £ ☐

£20 + £5 → £ ☐   £10 + £2 → £ ☐   £10 + £1 → £ ☐

C

Make these amounts. Use the number of notes and coins shown.

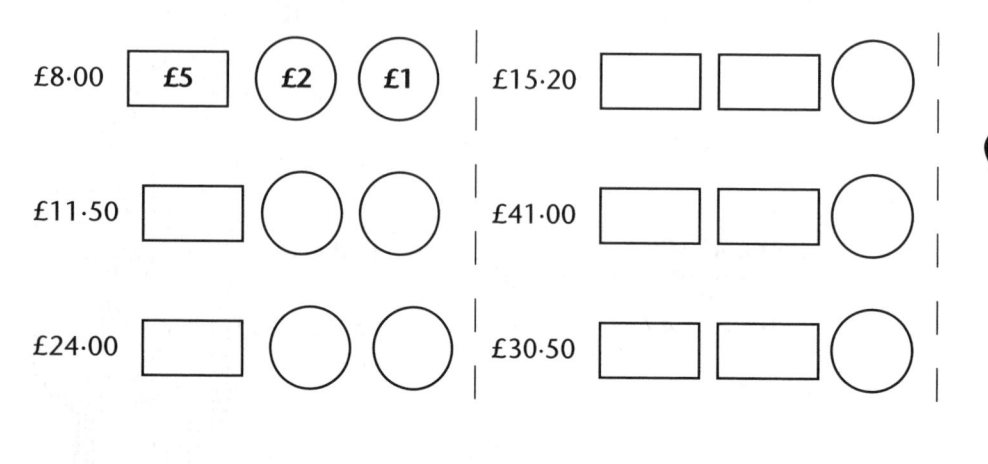

£8·00 £5 £2 £1   £15·20 ☐ ☐ ○

£11·50 ☐ ○ ○   £41·00 ☐ ☐ ○

£24·00 ☐ ○ ○   £30·50 ☐ ☐ ○

Sheet 61 POSITIONS

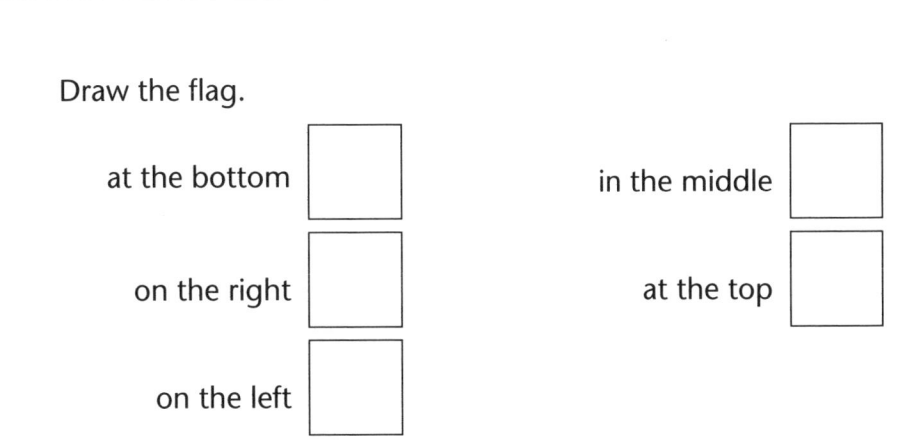

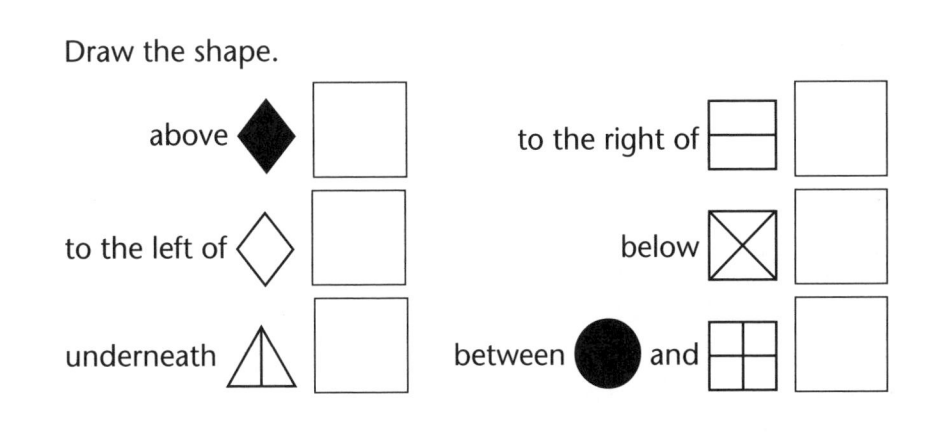

A

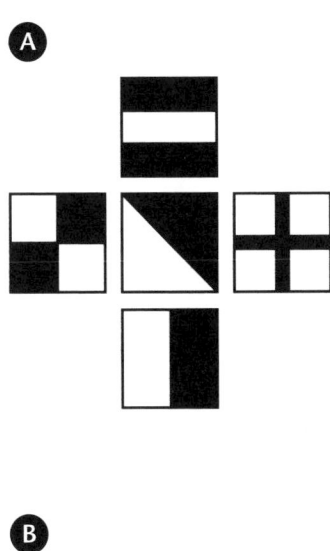

Draw the flag.

at the bottom ☐   in the middle ☐

on the right ☐   at the top ☐

on the left ☐

B

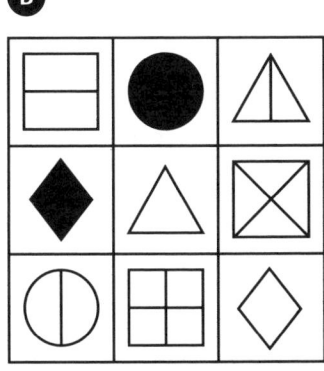

Draw the shape.

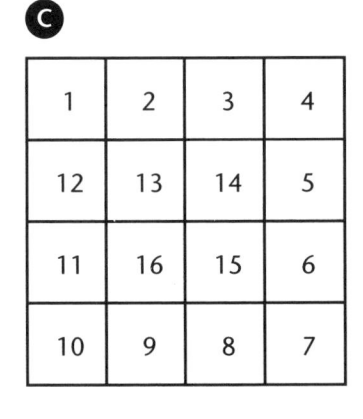

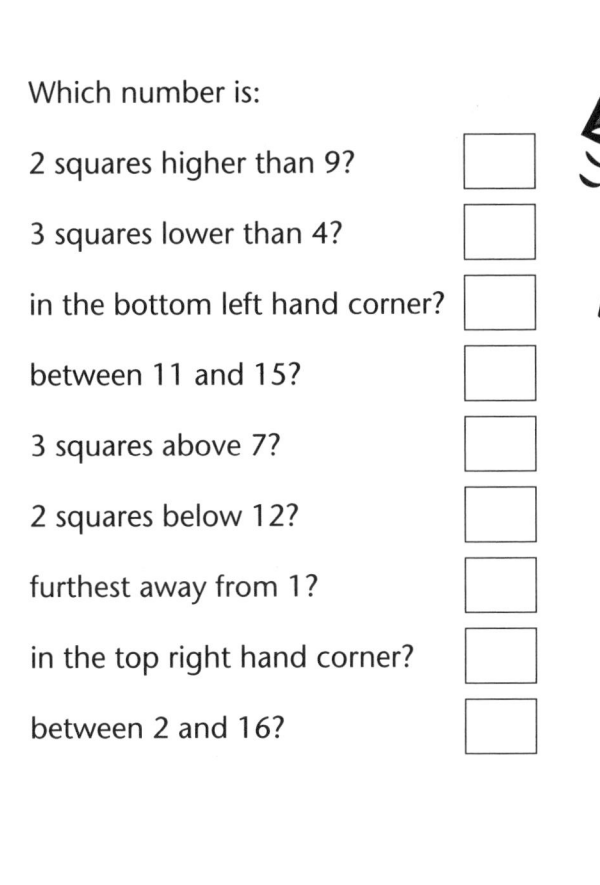

above ◆ ☐   to the right of ▭ ☐

to the left of ◇ ☐   below ⊠ ☐

underneath △ ☐   between ● and ⊞ ☐

C

1	2	3	4
12	13	14	5
11	16	15	6
10	9	8	7

Which number is:

2 squares higher than 9? ☐

3 squares lower than 4? ☐

in the bottom left hand corner? ☐

between 11 and 15? ☐

3 squares above 7? ☐

2 squares below 12? ☐

furthest away from 1? ☐

in the top right hand corner? ☐

between 2 and 16? ☐

Sheet 62 DIRECTIONS

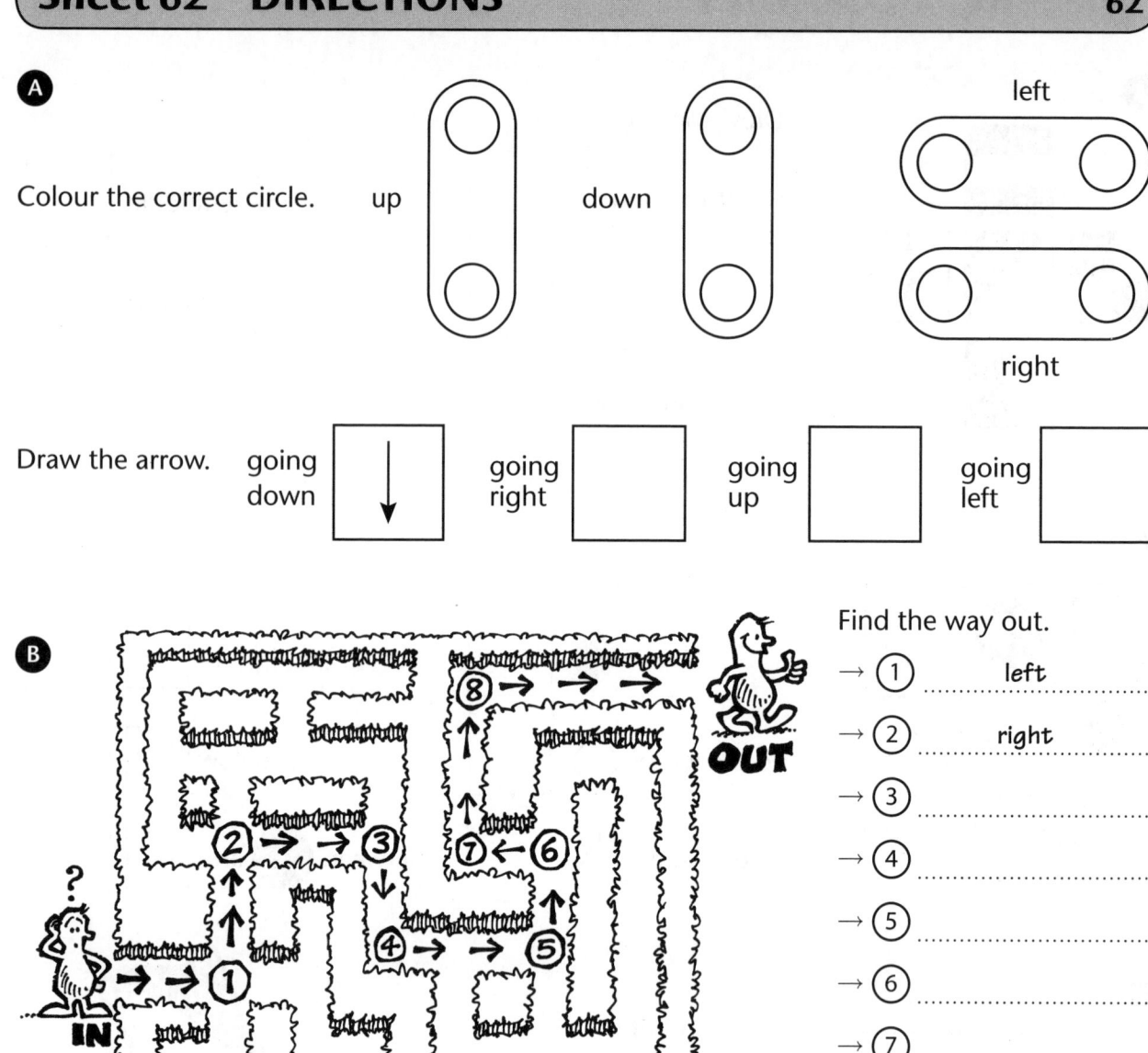

A

Colour the correct circle.   up   down   left / right

Draw the arrow.   going down [↓]   going right [ ]   going up [ ]   going left [ ]

B

Find the way out.

→ ① left
→ ② right
→ ③ ....
→ ④ ....
→ ⑤ ....
→ ⑥ ....
→ ⑦ ....
→ ⑧ ....

C

7	8	9	10
6	1	2	11
5	4	3	12
16	15	14	13

Start at 16. Up 3. Right 2. Finish at 9.

Start at 14. Up 2. Left 2. Finish at [ ].

Start at 10. Down 3. Left 3. Finish at [ ].

Start at 9. Down 2. Left 1. Finish at [ ].

Start at 6. Down 1. Right 3. Finish at [ ].

Start at 5. Up 1. Right 2. Finish at [ ].

Sheet 63 TURNS

A

Draw the hand on the clock after making one half turn.

B

Draw the hand after making the turn shown.

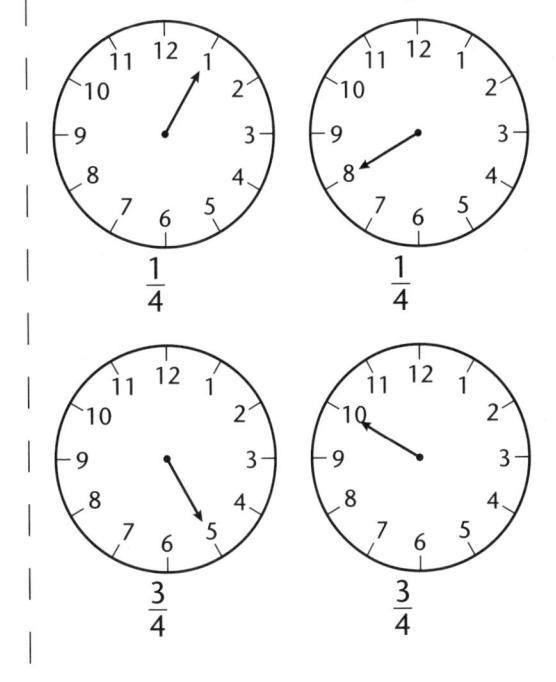

$\frac{1}{2}$ $\frac{3}{4}$

$\frac{1}{4}$ $\frac{1}{4}$

Draw the shape after making the clockwise turn shown.

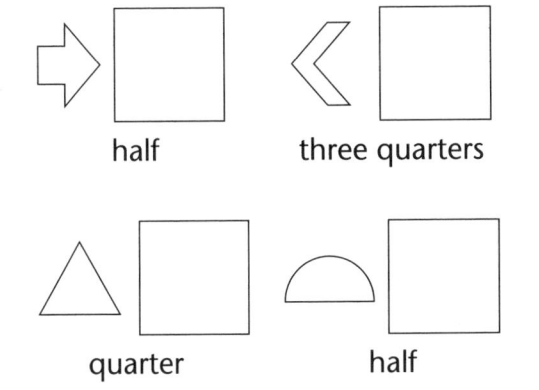

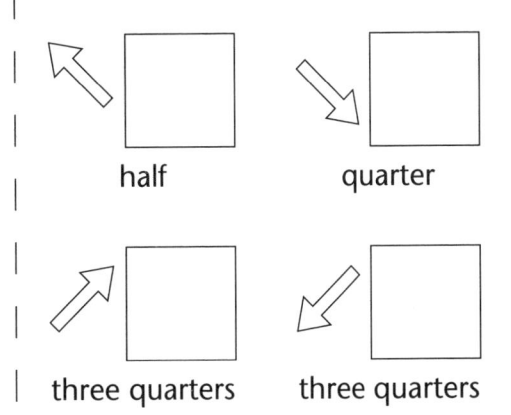

half   three quarters

quarter   half

C

Draw the hand after making the turn shown.

$\frac{1}{4}$ $\frac{1}{4}$

$\frac{3}{4}$ $\frac{3}{4}$

Draw the shape after making the clockwise turn shown.

half   quarter

three quarters   three quarters

Sheet 64 DOUBLING AND HALVING

Fill in both boxes with the same number.

A

3 + 3 = [6]

Double 3 = [6]

6 + 6 = [ ]

Double 6 = [ ]

1 + 1 = [ ]

Double 1 = [ ]

4 + 4 = [ ]

Double 4 = [ ]

B

7 + 7 = [ ]

Double 7 = [ ]

20 + 20 = [ ]

Double 20 = [ ]

9 + 9 = [ ]

Double 9 = [ ]

50 + 50 = [ ]

Double 50 = [ ]

C

35 + 35 = [ ]

Double 35 = [ ]

400 + 400 = [ ]

Double 400 = [ ]

16 + 16 = [ ]

Double 16 = [ ]

150 + 150 = [ ]

Double 150 = [ ]

Fill in all three boxes with the same number.

A

6 − [3] = [3]

Half of 6 = [3]

10 − [ ] = [ ]

Half of 10 = [ ]

4 − [ ] = [ ]

Half of 4 = [ ]

12 − [ ] = [ ]

Half of 12 = [ ]

B

14 − [ ] = [ ]

Half of 14 = [ ]

100 − [ ] = [ ]

Half of 100 = [ ]

20 − [ ] = [ ]

Half of 20 = [ ]

50 − [ ] = [ ]

Half of 50 = [ ]

C

24 − [ ] = [ ]

Half of 24 = [ ]

1000 − [ ] = [ ]

Half of 1000 = [ ]

30 − [ ] = [ ]

Half of 30 = [ ]

400 − [ ] = [ ]

Half of 400 = [ ]

Sheet 65 MULTIPLYING PROBLEMS

Fill in the boxes.

A

How many fingers on 2 hands?

Answer ☐ fingers

How many sausages in 2 pans?

Answer ☐ sausages

How many cakes on 2 plates?

Answer ☐ cakes

B

How many legs on 3 chairs?

Answer ☐ legs

How many cherries on 5 stalks?

Answer ☐

How much are four 5p coins?

Answer ☐ p

How many fish in 2 tanks?

Answer ☐

C

8 rolls in one pack.
5 packs.

☐ rolls altogether.

Three 20g weights.

☐ g total weight.

7 days in each week.
10 weeks.

☐ days altogether.

12 chairs in a row.
5 rows.

☐ chairs altogether.

Sheet 66   DIVIDING PROBLEMS

A

Use colours to share equally. Fill in the boxes.

10 fish.
2 bowls.

[ ] fish in each bowl.

8 sweets.
4 friends.

[ ] sweets each.

6 cakes.
3 plates.

[ ] cake each plate.

B

12 apples.
3 bowls.

[ ] apples in each bowl.

60p.
2 purses.

[ ] p in each purse.

15 pencils.
5 colours.

[ ] pencils of each colour.

12 cakes.
4 boxes.

[ ] cakes in each box.

C

18 shoes.
How many pairs?

Answer [ ] pairs.

40 books.
5 piles.

[ ] books in each pile.

30 children.
5 tables.

[ ] children at each table.

80 g.
10 g weights only.

[ ] weights.

Sheet 67 FRACTIONS OF QUANTITIES 1

A
Share the circles equally between 2 colours.

B
Colour half of the circles. Fill in the box.

$\frac{1}{2}$ of 4 ☐

$\frac{1}{2}$ of 12 ☐

$\frac{1}{2}$ of 18 ☐

$\frac{1}{2}$ of 20 ☐

$\frac{1}{2}$ of 8 ☐

C
Colour $\frac{1}{4}$ red. Colour $\frac{3}{4}$ blue.

$\frac{1}{4}$ of 8 ☐
$\frac{3}{4}$ of 8 ☐

$\frac{1}{4}$ of 16 ☐
$\frac{3}{4}$ of 16 ☐

$\frac{1}{4}$ of 12 ☐
$\frac{3}{4}$ of 12 ☐

$\frac{1}{4}$ of 24 ☐
$\frac{3}{4}$ of 24 ☐

Sheet 68 FRACTIONS OF QUANTITIES 2

A
Colour one half of the circles.
Fill in the box.

$\frac{1}{2}$ of 14 ☐

$\frac{1}{2}$ of 12 ☐

$\frac{1}{2}$ of 18 ☐

$\frac{1}{2}$ of 10 ☐

$\frac{1}{2}$ of 24 ☐

B
Colour one half red.
Colour one quarter blue.
Fill in the boxes.

$\frac{1}{2}$ of 16 ☐
$\frac{1}{4}$ of 16 ☐

$\frac{1}{2}$ of 8 ☐
$\frac{1}{4}$ of 8 ☐

$\frac{1}{2}$ of 24 ☐
$\frac{1}{4}$ of 24 ☐

$\frac{1}{2}$ of 20 ☐
$\frac{1}{4}$ of 20 ☐

C
Fill in the boxes.

$\frac{1}{2}$ of 12 ☐
$\frac{1}{4}$ of 12 ☐

$\frac{1}{2}$ of 40 ☐
$\frac{1}{4}$ of 40 ☐

$\frac{1}{2}$ of 16 ☐
$\frac{1}{4}$ of 16 ☐

$\frac{1}{2}$ of 60 ☐
$\frac{1}{4}$ of 60 ☐

$\frac{1}{2}$ of 4p ☐ p
$\frac{1}{4}$ of 4p ☐ p

$\frac{1}{2}$ of 20 cm ☐ cm
$\frac{1}{4}$ of 20 cm ☐ cm

$\frac{1}{2}$ of 80p ☐ p
$\frac{1}{4}$ of 80p ☐ p

$\frac{1}{2}$ of 100 cm ☐ cm
$\frac{1}{4}$ of 100 cm ☐ cm

Sheet 69 MISSING NUMBER PROBLEMS 2

Fill in the boxes.

A

5 + [2] = 7   [9] − 6 = 3   10 − [ ] = 7

2 + [ ] = 9   [ ] − 9 = 1   7 − [ ] = 3

4 + [ ] = 10   [ ] − 5 = 1   5 − [ ] = 4

1 + [ ] = 6   [ ] − 4 = 4   8 − [ ] = 8

3 + [ ] = 8   [ ] − 1 = 6   10 − [ ] = 2

B

4 + [ ] = 13   [ ] − 5 = 11   18 − [ ] = 4

8 + [ ] = 16   [ ] − 8 = 4   12 − [ ] = 5

5 + [ ] = 17   [ ] − 17 = 3   15 − [ ] = 6

14 + [ ] = 20   [ ] − 9 = 8   14 − [ ] = 7

7 + [ ] = 11   [ ] − 6 = 7   20 − [ ] = 8

C

9 + [ ] = 47   [ ] − 40 = 40   63 − [ ] = 53

26 + [ ] = 31   [ ] − 83 = 8   100 − [ ] = 70

40 + [ ] = 60   [ ] − 28 = 6   78 − [ ] = 0

78 + [ ] = 85   [ ] − 50 = 50   90 − [ ] = 20

16 + [ ] = 24   [ ] − 9 = 56   52 − [ ] = 4

Sheet 70 +/− PROBLEMS 2

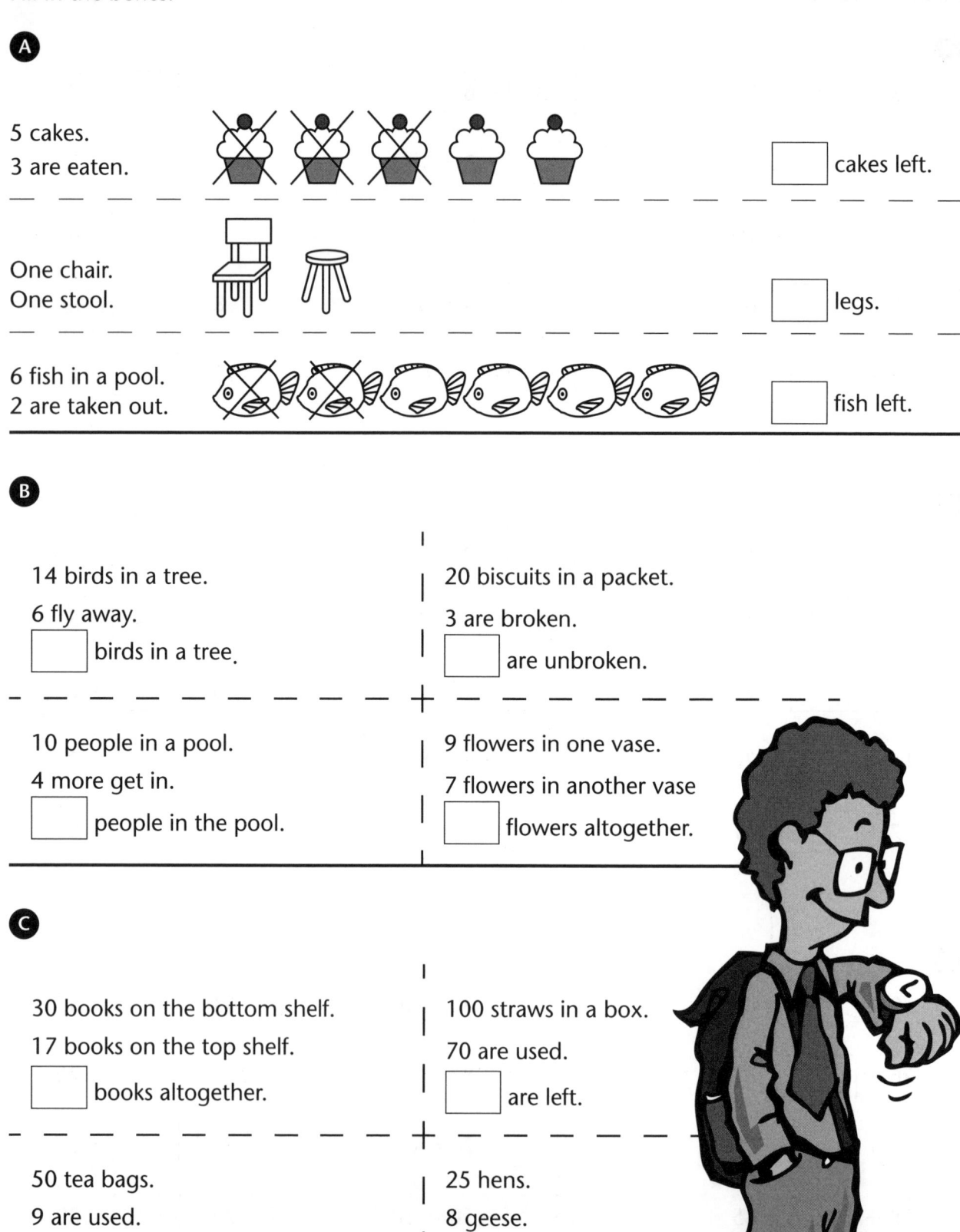

Fill in the boxes.

A

5 cakes.
3 are eaten.
☐ cakes left.

One chair.
One stool.
☐ legs.

6 fish in a pool.
2 are taken out.
☐ fish left.

B

14 birds in a tree.
6 fly away.
☐ birds in a tree.

20 biscuits in a packet.
3 are broken.
☐ are unbroken.

10 people in a pool.
4 more get in.
☐ people in the pool.

9 flowers in one vase.
7 flowers in another vase
☐ flowers altogether.

C

30 books on the bottom shelf.
17 books on the top shelf.
☐ books altogether.

100 straws in a box.
70 are used.
☐ are left.

50 tea bags.
9 are used.
☐ tea bags left.

25 hens.
8 geese.
☐ birds.

Sheet 71 CLOCKS 2

Draw the hands on the clocks.

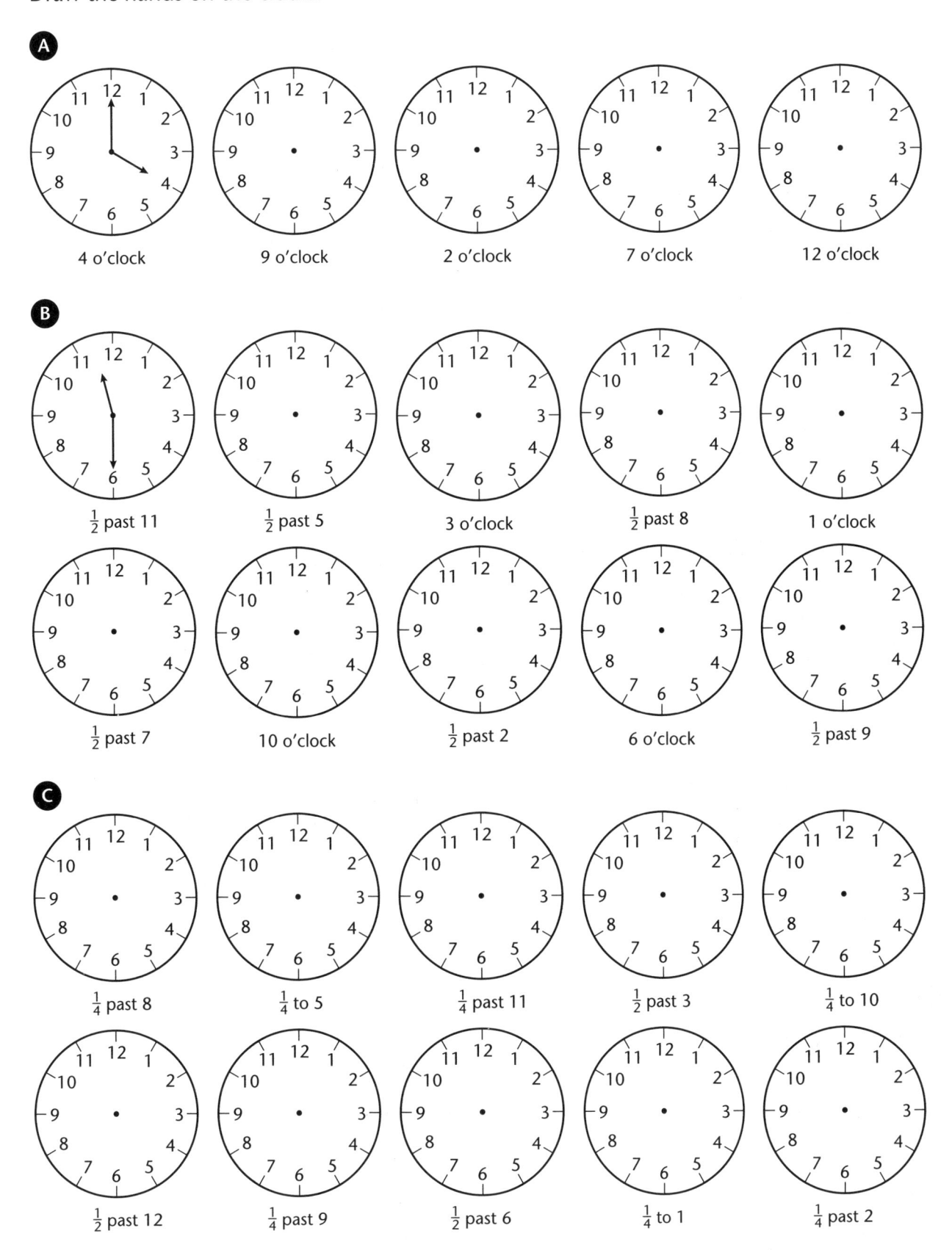

A

4 o'clock   9 o'clock   2 o'clock   7 o'clock   12 o'clock

B

½ past 11   ½ past 5   3 o'clock   ½ past 8   1 o'clock

½ past 7   10 o'clock   ½ past 2   6 o'clock   ½ past 9

C

¼ past 8   ¼ to 5   ¼ past 11   ½ past 3   ¼ to 10

½ past 12   ¼ past 9   ½ past 6   ¼ to 1   ¼ past 2

Sheet 72   COMPARING TIMES

A

Write the time one hour:

earlier ⏰ later

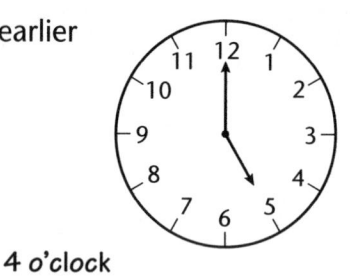

4 o'clock ....

earlier ⏰ later

....

earlier ⏰ later

....

earlier ⏰ later

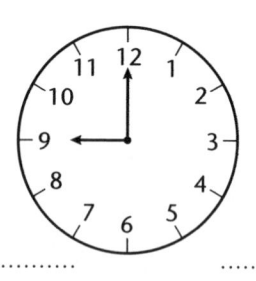

....

B

Write the time:

30 minutes earlier ⏰ 30 minutes later

....

1 hour earlier ⏰ 1 hour later

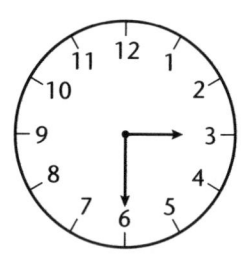

....

30 minutes earlier ⏰ 1 hour later

....

1 hour earlier ⏰ 1 hour later

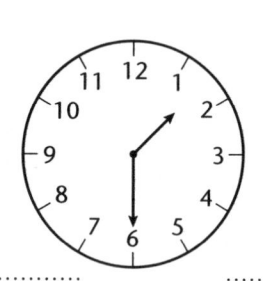

....

C

The time is quarter past 3.
Write the time:

30 minutes later   ....

1 hour earlier   ....

45 minutes later   ....

15 minutes earlier   ....

The time is quarter to 1.
Write the time:

30 minutes earlier   ....

1 hour later   ....

45 minutes earlier   ....

15 minutes later   ....